The Feedback Loop:
Historians Talk about the Links between Research and Teaching

The Feedback Loop:
Historians Talk about the Links between Research and Teaching

Edited by Antoinette M. Burton

with essays by
Antoinette M. Burton, Teofilo F. Ruiz, Steve Johnstone,
Carol Symes, Shefali Chandra, Laura E. Nym Mayhall,
Mary Jo Maynes and Ann Waltner, Bianca Premo,
Kathi Kern, John Ramsbottom, Jennifer L. Morgan,
Catherine Ceniza Choy, Lisa A. Lindsay,
and Jeffrey Wasserstrom

Produced by the American Historical Association

AHA Editors: Robert B. Townsend and Allen Mikaelian

Layout and Cover Design: Christian A. Hale

© 2013 by the American Historical Association

ISBN: 978-0-87229-203-1

All rights reserved. No part of this book may be reproduced in any form without permission in writing from the publisher, except by a reviewer who wishes to quote brief passages in connection with a review written for inclusion in a magazine or newspaper.

Published in 2013 by the American Historical Association. As publisher, the American Historical Association does not adopt official views on any field of history and does not necessarily agree or disagree with the views expressed in this book.

Library of Congress Cataloging-in-Publication Data:

The feedback loop : historians talk about the links between research and teaching / edited by Antoinette M. Burton ; with essays by Antoinette M. Burton, Teofilo F. Ruiz, Steve Johnstone, Carol Symes, Shefali Chandra, Laura E. Nym Mayhall, Mary Jo Maynes and Ann Waltner, Bianca Premo, Kathi Kern, John Ramsbottom, Jennifer L. Morgan, Catherine Ceniza Choy, Lisa A. Lindsay, and Jeffrey Wasserstrom.

pages cm

Includes bibliographical references and index.

ISBN 978-0-87229-203-1 (alk. paper)

1. Historiography—Methodology. 2. History—Research. 3. History—Study and teaching. 4. History teachers—Training of. I. Burton, Antoinette M., 1961– author, editor of compilation. II. American Historical Association, issuing body.

D16.F44 2013   907.2--dc23   2013017477

Contents

Introduction: The Feedback Loop—Fact and Friction
Antoinette M. Burton 1

Teaching as Research / Research as Teaching
Teofilo F. Ruiz 7

Of Doubt
Steve Johnstone 15

The Shakespeare Teacher: Shakespeare's Globe and the Prisoner's World
Carol Symes 21

Global India and the Divergent Temporalities of South Asia
Shefali Chandra 29

Teaching our Process: How Research Shapes My Teaching
Laura E. Nym Mayhall 35

Doing "Our Own Work," As Undergraduate Teachers
Mary Jo Maynes and Ann Waltner 41

The List: What Students Should Know about Federally Funded Historical Research
Bianca Premo 47

Teaching in the Archive: What the Professor Learned
Kathi Kern 55

"Spare the Messenger": Envisioning a Future for Teacher-Historians
John Ramsbottom 63

Race and Feminisms in Slavery's Archive
Jennifer L. Morgan 69

Pedagogical Crossroads: On Teaching and Conducting Research in Asian American History
Catherine Ceniza Choy 75

The African Diaspora and the Political Imagination
Lisa A. Lindsay 83

Bringing Communication Back In: Rethinking the Teaching-Research-Service Distinction
Jeffrey Wasserstrom 89

About the Authors 93

Introduction
The Feedback Loop: Fact and Friction

Antoinette Burton

When I first came across the speech made by English MP Handel Cossham to protest the second Anglo-Afghan war (1878–80), I wasn't, frankly, expecting much. Trawling the collections of the British Library as part of a trip to London in fall 2010 to research a new project about resistance to the British Empire, I had turned up masses of material on both the second and the first Anglo-Afghan wars (the first fought from 1839–42), and was now making my way through soldiers' memoirs and related ephemera. Most of the material I looked into lay in the main reading room of the British Library, but the Cossham speech, bundled in with other pamphlets from the period, was viewable only in the manuscript room due to its fragile binding. So I decamped down the hallway with my pad and pencil and sat down to see what the MP from Bath had had to say.

I could not believe how modern his case sounded. "My countrymen," Cossham declaimed, "this war can bring us naught but dishonor and disgrace; it was begun it the dark, has been planned and pursued under the guise of deception and falsehood; it is unjust in its aims and will be ruinous in its results." His speech rehearses the pros and cons and quotes extensively from political debates leading up to the second Afghan war that, like the one before it, was a military campaign fought in the name of global imperial security. Cossham takes aim at a host of aristocrats, including Lord Beaconsfield (Benjamin Disraeli, whose second ministry lasted from 1874 to 1880), and allows us to see, in the process, the long tradition of war as a political as well as a military issue. Afghanistan in 1878 was part and parcel of the "great game" in Central Asia that the British had been playing with Russia for decades, a fact to which Cossham frequently alludes.

As a Liberal Party member, Cossham wanted to win that game every bit as much as his Tory colleagues across the aisle. Yet, given Britain's posture at the Congress of Berlin (also 1878), where the Great Powers professed a commitment to peace and stability, he feared that British involvement in Afghanistan showed "our hypocrisy and selfishness and subtlety have been exposed before the whole world." Cossham was a colliery-owner as well as an MP, but it's hard to know exactly how or why that disposed him to oppose the war. Mid-century liberals like Richard Cobden had been anti-war even as they were pro-empire, so his stance resonated as part of a broader liberal-imperial formation. For Cossham, the enduring question remained the cost of unnecessary war in Afghanistan: in his view, "the national disgrace, the shame" was to be found "in the crime of spilling blood uselessly."

I am sure I interrupted the sepulchral hush of the manuscript room—where no one speaks above a whisper and there is an air of high seriousness one normally associates with sacred venues—with gasps of recognition and astonishment. (Happily, no one seemed to notice.) So many of Cossham's arguments, his vocabulary even, sound contemporary—as if some Victorians had anticipated the claims that would be made by those who opposed the Afghan and Iraq wars at the beginning of our own century. We learn that Tories like Lord Bury "explain and defend" this campaign as a "just and necessary war"—a phrase that leaps out for its contemporary resonance. Cossham's speech recounts his local alderman's case for war in Afghanistan on the grounds that it is a "defensive" strategy. "May I ask the worthy Alderman to tell me[,] if this is a 'defensive' war[,] whoever engaged in an aggressive war? We go into a neighbour's territory who has not attacked us, who has done us no wrong, we seize his strongholds, desolate his country, murder his subjects, and seek to take his capital, and then roll our pious eyes up and thank God we are only engaged in a 'defensive war.'" Reading such prose one century and a half on reminds me of why I became a historian: not simply to make "discoveries" but to appreciate how profoundly we are connected to the past, even when its particulars differ. My only regret was being so far from home that I had no one with whom to share the immediate experience.

As I reflected on how deeply the document before me resonated with my project and with the headlines of the day, I began to think about how I might use what I had found in my classrooms at the University of Illinois at Urbana-Champaign. I'd been teaching a unit on the Anglo-Afghan wars in my upper-level Victorian Britain course since 9/11, but I had little primary documentation to share with students, in part because battle per se had not been my area of interest or specialty. Since beginning my current project on militarism and the British Empire, I've discovered volumes of ink that Victorians dispensed on remembering and arguing about these two 19th-century conflicts on the northwest frontier (and many others besides). As I gathered more primary material, I began to develop ideas for a more elaborate class session on the wars, with Cossham at the center.

A year after finding his speech in the British Library, I was teaching it to a class of juniors, seniors, and graduate students. We spent a class session in mid-September 2011 thinking through his arguments—both in terms of their resonance with current events and their historical meaning for the late 1870s—just as headlines announcing an attack on the British Council in Kabul and myriad other "post-occupation" crises swirled around the US mainstream media. In History 448, students worked with a Xerox copy of Cossham's speech tracked down via interlibrary loan through Illinois' wonderful library system (the British Library wouldn't copy the version I read initially because it was too vulnerable to disintegration). This meant that students could see the typeface of the 1878 pamphlet and get a mediated yet Victorian feel from the text itself.

Students appeared as astonished as I by the contemporaneity of Cossham's prose and the reasons he believed the war an unwise course of action. "If so many people were against the war," one student asked, "how did it happen?" They were also amazed to realize how much of the debate as a whole—pro and con—they could reconstruct using the extensive passages Cossham cites from parliamentary debate and other speeches. At the most basic level, they were surprised to learn that previous wars had been waged in the "graveyard of empires," since their history training thus far had not brought them into contact with these antecedents to our own involvement in the region. Confronted with evidence of the utter failure of these earlier campaigns—i.e., in the face of "tribal" fighters who confounded apparently "superior" British military technology—one student marveled at the lack of historical knowledge on the part of those in charge of 21st-century operations. Seemingly, he suggested, "no one did the research."

We commented too on Cossham's lack of attention to Afghani dead, though our other readings made the agency of tribesmen and indigenous people of the region evident. All of this gave me an opportunity at the end of class to talk about the histories of this region, and how many of those books our library has—whether new works or 19th-century accounts. I also spoke with students about my own research, and described how I found Cossham's speech in the British Library and eventually made it available online in the e-reserve section of our own library. I took the opportunity to talk as well about what it means to be a student of history in a institution like Illinois, where faculty have the privilege of sharing their scholarly projects directly with students either in the form of a course topic, a lecture, or a primary document like Cossham's. And I hope to persuade some, who are seniors, to do their own research projects on an aspect of one or both of the Victorian wars using our rich collection of periodical and printed materials on the subject.

The idea for *The Feedback Loop* was motivated in part by the experience I've just described. Most historians undoubtedly have such tales to tell, even allowing for the diversity of research topics, archives, and language/translation issues. And, of course, we are as interested in what marks us off from the past as we are in what sutures then and now—a dialectic shaped by our geographical specialties and periods as well as by how our intellectual interests and commitments shift and change over the course of our careers as teachers and scholars and institutional citizens. But we rarely talk about them, nor are we encouraged to do so in a profession that still places a premium on research and tends to subordinate teaching as a vocation, particularly where writing is concerned. Though there may be little precedent and even less institutional will for it, this is exactly why the contributions to this collection should count in annual reports, or whatever constitutes the basis for salary consideration in our contributors' home institutions. Writing about teaching is, or should be, part of what historians do—both for how it reflects their research and for how it might re-orient or nuance it as well. For symbolic and material reasons, then, *The Feedback Loop* is an effort to illustrate the payoffs of this kind of work, and to jump start conversation about the disconnect between the domains of research and teaching in ways that effect debates about best practices as well as questions of value, status, and merit.

This collection has also been summoned by contemporary pressures—a historical moment when the use-value of a liberal arts education is in question and the relevance of a history degree is something about which parents and taxpayers remain hyper-vigilant. Research and teaching in the humanities (as elsewhere) is under threat from a variety of quarters, requiring us to justify our roles as researchers at the expense of our work as teachers and vice versa. Historians in particular are being asked to redefine their roles in the liberal arts educational schemes of the 21st century at a moment when the competition for students and the uncertain fate of tertiary education *tout court* requires all educators to specify their intellectual, political, and ethical obligations to their craft and to a variety of publics in historically unprecedented ways. My call for papers for this volume sought contributors who were willing to write about the tense and tender relationships between teaching and research in their own institutional settings, while contributing to conversations in the profession and beyond that engage these kinds of questions.

The results include essays by historians from various spaces in higher education in the United States reflecting on what they see as the relationship between research and teaching in their own professional practice. In this context, the feedback loop metaphor is heuristic rather than predictive. Some have traced the literal connections between various aspects of research practice, from form to content, and their syllabi and classroom assignments (Ruiz, Lindsay, Chandra, Johnstone, Waltner, and Maynes). Others have mapped the way these connections exceed the walls of the classroom, virtual and otherwise—propelling them into some of the most critical social and political issues of the day (Premo, Symes and Morgan). Still others dig deep, modeling best practices at the conceptual and the cellular level (Choy, Kern and Mayhall). Just as important, some have taken direct issue with the question of what stands in the way of a smooth or easy "loop" between research and teaching (Ramsbottom, Wasserstrom).

Of course, no one essay fits neatly into any one of these categories. Indeed, it's striking how much evidence of friction contributors reveal as they engage with the idea of a feedback loop. This is hardly surprising, given the nature of the contemporary political economy of higher education in which historians in North America labor. Understanding its genealogies and its current practices are of critical importance if we are to (re)position history as a critical resource for the worlds of the 21st century. I recognize, too, that these are exclusively American stories. They should impel us to consider the impact of our own locative positions on our professional experiences—something that historians who teach and research parts of the world outside North America grapple with on a regular basis, even as all of us who work in the United States are shaped by the categorical assumptions of its higher education framework.

Of special note in these essays is evidence of the myriad ways in which our students impact our teaching, propelling us back to our first principles, pushing the limits of our empirical knowledge, and surprising us with startling combinations of insight and re-orientation that serve as the spark for new pedagogies and new research questions. That is a humbling reminder of why the relationship between teaching and research, whether smooth or fractious, requires greater attention if we are to think more than impressionistically about when, how, and under what conditions history is made. Those conditions include not just the rhetorical and political fallout from global fiscal crises, but also the corollary rise of the adjunct instructor as the fate of the future historian-teacher/historian-researcher. As for my own experience, if Cossham's speech gives depth to the headline news that Illinois students glance at, or propels them to seek more knowledge about Kabul and Kandahar, or just sheds a glancing light on the links between past and present, then they will have had some experience of how the feedback loop between research and teaching operates. And I plan to keep their classroom responses alive in my own work to ensure that the pathways between research and teaching run in both directions.

Teaching as Research/ Research as Teaching

Teofilo F. Ruiz

Teaching as Research

Allow me to begin with a personal note and a story. When I am asked, "What is that you do?" I never describe myself as a researcher or a writer, even though in my very long academic career I have published 14 books and over 70 articles. Nonetheless, to that question my answer is always the same: "I am a teacher." This is what I do, and what I am. Such an assertion does not mean that I reject or neglect my research. Rather, it means that my identity as a scholar is embedded in my life as a teacher and in my role as an educator, mentor, advocate, and friend to my students. I recently completed a tour as one of last year's Phi Beta Kappa lecturers. Along with the others selected for this great honor, I have traveled the United States, visiting PBK chapters and lecturing in undergraduate classes, usually in small liberal arts colleges. During the academic year 2011–12, I visited seven universities and colleges in Missouri, Massachusetts, Maryland, Pennsylvania, and Virginia. It has been an exciting and rewarding experience. But it has been so, first and foremost, because of the opportunity that these visits have provided me for witnessing and experiencing firsthand the commitment that these teachers—all of them in a wide variety of settings, from large research universities to small private liberal arts colleges—devote to their students and their teaching.

Although this was my experience wherever I visited, the example of the faculty at Randolph Macon College, Amherst College, Washington College, Virginia Tech, Haverford College, St. Louis University, and Villanova University have left an indelible mark on my long appreciation of, and interest in, teaching. It was also clear to me that even though I was not always fully familiar with the publications or research record of my hosts, they were all deeply committed to research as an integral part of their teaching.

While I do not wish to sound sanctimonious or too idealistic, teaching is or ought to be a calling. As I once wrote in another context: to be truly human is to teach and to be taught. And yet, American teachers endure numerous jokes at their expense, as well as outright hostility from local governments and much of the general public. We teach, of course, for many different reasons, but I have always found Bernard de Clairvaux's (a 12th-century Cistercian monk, saint, and mystic) definition of the pursuit of knowledge, and the transmission of that knowledge, to be one of the most compelling statements about what is that we do:

> There are many who seek knowledge for the sake of knowledge; that is curiosity. There are others who desire to know in order that they may themselves be known: that is vanity. Others seek knowledge in order to sell it; that is dishonorable. But there are also some who seek knowledge in order to edify others: that is love [*caritas*]. And again there are still others who seek knowledge in order to be edified: that is prudence.[1]

I think that most of you reading this essay would agree that we have embraced a life as teachers mostly for what Bernard defined as *caritas* (love) or in search of what Bernard defined as prudence. The two are closely linked. After all, to be a good and effective teacher more is required than just empathy or love for our students. We cannot be effective teachers unless we continuously work to keep our courses fresh. That requires us to read widely in the fields related to the topics we teach, and to interpret and explicate primary sources to our students according to the latest methodological trends. Innovative teachers are always driven by their curiosity and willingness to explore a diversity of approaches to and interpretations of any topic. If we were to teach the same course again and again without continuously revising our information and trying out new historiographical approaches, we would be doing a great disservice to our students and, most of all, to ourselves.

The history I learned 40 years ago in undergraduate and graduate courses in my own field of research and teaching (the Middle Ages) is very different from the history I write or teach today. Over the last four decades, fundamental shifts in the topics we teach and how we teach them, along with new educational technologies—computers, PowerPoint, web-based learning tools—have transformed the classroom. When I began my career, trained as I was in the kind of institutional history still popular at Princeton under the much-loved Joseph R. Strayer, I taught courses that emphasized the politics of the Middle Ages, the rise of embryonic states, and topics that revolved around institutional structures. My geographical focus was on the core regions of medieval western Europe, mostly England and France, neglecting the periphery.

As I developed as a historian, and came to embrace the influence of the new social history and the history of mentalities—inspired by Lawrence Stone at the Davis Center at Princeton, Clifford Geertz at the Institute for Advanced Study, and Jacques Le Goff at the École des hautes études in Paris—my teaching and writing changed radically to incorporate those new ways of perceiving, researching, and teaching the past. Recent trends in cultural history have found their way into my most recent book on festivals as well as into the courses I have taught on the relationship between popular and elite culture and performance. At the same time, my research interests and teaching have moved to areas once considered peripheral to western Europe and to the western Mediterranean.

Far more important in dictating what and how we teach is the reality that our students differ substantially from students of 40, 30, and even 5 years ago. The present generation of students is the first cohort to have grown up entirely in an environment of e-mail and the World Wide Web. We often decry their lack of preparation, their dependence on electronic gadgets, on Wikipedia, and the things they do not know—but of course they also know things that many of us, certainly myself, know not at all or only vaguely. It is not that they do not know anything, but that they know different things and learn them very differently.

If I were to teach the same courses I have taught for almost 40 years, in the same fashion I did then, I would be betraying my students by conveying to them information or interpretative approaches that are no longer valid or that been either rejected or radically transformed by four decades of scholarship. I would also go mad with sheer tedium. Thus, I offer here some suggestions on how to connect research and teaching based upon my own experiences.

> **Keep in touch with the new scholarship in one's field.**
> While only a handful of very gifted scholars are able to read everything, mere mortals, among whom I most certainly count myself, can keep abreast of methodological developments by reading reviews, keeping a hand on recently published

scholarship directly related to one's courses. These new scholarly contributions may hold the key to the possibility of saying something new and interesting to our students. This type of research—closely related to teaching, not necessarily resulting in publications—should be fostered and rewarded by departments and institutions. The National Endowment for the Humanities (NEH) runs summer seminars and institutes geared specifically to re-invigorating teachers, exploring new topics, developing new courses, and providing opportunities for research not aimed at publication. A recurring NEH Institute in Barcelona focuses on the western Mediterranean and has successfully introduced young and old scholars to new historical problems and methodologies. While the NEH has fallen victim to the fiscal crisis (as have most academic organizations in the country), our own institutions, our own departments, need to promote workshops and gatherings that encourage new research as the basis for innovative teaching.

Use different course materials. I always like to try at least one new and/or different book in each of my classes and to assign different primary sources from quarter to quarter, avoiding the temptation to assign the same books and readings year after year. Request for syllabi and reading lists have an unfortunate tendency to come at the wrong time every term. They appear on our computer screens when we are barely able to think. Plan ahead! See what works in the classroom and what does not; try something new. In the same vein, change the questions asked in your exams or the assignments for papers and projects.

Over my almost 40 years of teaching, I have always learned a great deal from exams and students' papers, which teach me to see specific topics from different perspectives. First, they allow me to judge what works in the classroom, what I need to explain better, and whether I should abandon certain topics in favor of others. Second, there are insights from both undergraduates and graduate students that make me revise my own views on specific subjects and influence my own research and publications. A terrific senior thesis on the impact of the Black Death on the inhabitants of Oxfordshire in 1348, as garnered from the documents in the *Calendar of the Close, Fine and Patent Rolls*, taught me vividly about the disconnect between our view of the pervasive impact of the plague and the normal rhythms of everyday life. A thoughtful graduate student's paper on translators in 16th-century North Africa found its way (with all proper attributions) into a forthcoming book on the western Mediterranean, leading me to explore an area of research that I had neglected in greater detail, and to incorporate new chapters on linguistic interlocutors into my book. These small, new approaches to teaching represent a form of research, of continuing to learn—even if that research does not translate into publication.

Teach new courses. I know that most of us often feel overwhelmed by the number of courses we teach and committees we are asked to serve (I certainly am), but teaching an entirely new course—whether graduate, undergraduate, or even outside of one's field—provides a sure way to learn something new and bring different perspectives into your regular courses. In fall 2010, for the first time in my life, I taught world history. The first part of our three-course sequence in world history, History 20 covers the beginning of life on earth to around 500 CE. It was one of the most exhilarating and memorable experiences in my life as a teacher. We often forget the thrill of learning as teachers: not only did I absorb new things about "big history"— Gilgamesh, India, China, the Buddha, and other topics that I either did not know or knew only superficially—but I also learned to teach Western civilization and the Middle Ages in a different manner than I had for nearly 40 years. Teaching that class has given me a comparative perspective that I now incorporate in most of my courses; it marked the high point of my life as a teacher. It also meant that I had to do research on topics far removed from my own area of specialization. That new knowledge has found its way into some of my recent publications, and I liked the class so very much that I have volunteered to do the entire sequence.

Try to engage students in new ways of learning. We should think beyond the lecture, discussion sections, traditional exams, and papers. Since I was a teaching assistant (or preceptor, as it was called) at Princeton, in a class taught by Carl Schorske (probably the greatest teacher I have ever seen), I have encouraged dramatic representations in my regular classes, as well as blogs or photographic journals in my Paris summer program. At Princeton in 1972, in a course on Vienna, the students in my section performed Schnitzler's *La Ronde*, a play that had been assigned to all the students. Witnessing the play performed by students provided an intellectual and aesthetic experience far superior to merely reading the play. Performing in it also greatly enhanced the experience.

In my Paris summer course, in addition to written essays, students create photographic essays or keep blogs about Parisian streets or material life. In my courses at UCLA, students have performed interpretative dances, music, plays, and other imaginative projects related to the period under study. I am often awed by my students' creativity, by how much they learn from imaginative activity, and by how much I learn as well. When they stand in front of their peers and recite parts of an early modern play, or sing medieval music, they are learning, but so are their fellow students. In History 20, two students performed a song that they had composed and put to music based on their reading of the Gita. It was one of the most moving experiences I have ever had in a classroom, and most of the other (400 plus) students were in tears, transformed by the experience. It was an epiphany for them and for me. And is not that what we aim to do in the classroom?

Research as Teaching

In the humanities and social sciences, and even in the sciences, research is always intended as a scholarly way of teaching. Those who read our books and articles may sometimes quarrel with this assertion, and we may write erudite monographic studies driven by intense archival research and intended for a narrow audience, addressed to a few scholars engaged in similar research. Having written some of those books, I know that their reach is often limited, and that such monographs seldom have an impact beyond a narrow audience of specialists and/or graduate seminars focused on specific topics related to the book's primary subject.

We may also write books offering synthetic views of particular periods or problems in history. We aim these books not just to scholars but hope to address the general public as well. I recently published a book dedicated to my students and entitled *The Terror of History* that sought, above all, to answer the queries articulated by numberless students over the last four decades. The book is built around students' questions about their lives, the ways we make meaning in the face of catastrophes, and what this all means in the end. They are the questions posed by students over two generations, but they are my questions as well.

Finally, we may write textbooks geared for first-year students. These different tiers of readers—narrow and scholarly, or directed to the general student population—parallel and replicate different levels of teaching: from the lower-division or general courses required of all students, to the upper-level electives intended for juniors and seniors, to the seminars (both graduate and undergraduate) aimed at a more sophisticated discussion of historiography and methodology.

Research—even published research—is by its nature an extension of our teaching. Research is evidence of pedagogical intent and is, above all, heuristic in nature. When we publish the fruits of our research or condense the knowledge of others into synthetic works, we are engaged in teaching beyond the physical confines of the classroom. The revolution in communication, the increase in the number of online courses, and the ability to teach seminars across geographical boundaries has transformed the classroom, the way we teach, and the way our students learn.

Our teaching, the result of research, can now be conveyed to large numbers of people in ways that were incomprehensible 15 or 20 years ago. I recorded an online class on Western civilization that was first offered in summer 2012. It was my first such venture. On the one hand, I fear the consequences of online teaching and what such courses will do to our profession; on the other hand, students—and this pertains to my remark about new ways of learning—yearn for these types of courses. One of my distinguished colleagues at UCLA, David Sabean, has been running a very successful graduate seminar that meets in Los Angeles, Zurich, and Tel Aviv. The students communicate via a sophisticated interactive television or Skype, and meet in person for one week at the end of their two-quarter seminar. Is that not the kind of innovative and new teaching we should be developing? These examples demonstrate that a great deal of accumulated research goes into these enterprises before they reach the hundreds of undergraduates or 30 graduate students in the form of teaching and transmitting knowledge.

To be a successful scholar, one must be able to articulate ideas in ways that are accessible to peers but also to young students and to the general public. Scholarly publications are always didactic in nature. Writers, researchers, would benefit immensely, as would their readers, by applying the pedagogical lessons derived from years of teaching to research publications.

Teaching helps me a great deal in formulating a research and publication agenda. There is very little in my books that I have not discussed or tried out in the classroom. Student reception of my interpretations and arguments helps me to refine and focus my own work. I rehearsed the material for a recent publication on late medieval and early modern Spanish festivals in three graduate seminars, and certain of the book's themes also found their way into my undergraduate lectures. How students reacted to my research and ideas helped me to refine and correct some of my mistakes. In many respects, I also write in the same manner I teach, seeking to incorporate the rhetorical elements and flourishes I deploy in the classroom into my oral or written presentations. After all, this is essentially what we do in many graduate seminars: air out problems that we are close to or wish to render into writing. Once again, in seminars and also in lecture courses, I have been led to change my mind, to formulate my ideas differently because of my students' comments, criticisms, and suggestions. How can we then think of research and teaching as distinct categories? Instead, they are two aspects of one enterprise: how we acquire knowledge, and how we then transmit it to our colleagues, students, and to the future. There is no statistical evidence that those restricted solely to "pure" research, without any teaching obligations—I am thinking of bodies such as the CNRS in France, the CSIC in Spain, and think-tanks and research institutes in the United States—are more productive or publish more than those for whom teaching is an integral and *necessary* part of their scholarly lives. There is, in fact, no valid teaching without research, and no research without teaching.

Of Doubt

Steve Johnstone

Beginning the story of the growth of imperial power in the eastern Mediterranean over two centuries and how the Persians came into conflict with the Greeks, Herodotus relates what Persians and Phoenicians say: The Phoenicians first abducted Io and the Greeks retaliated by kidnapping Europa, the Greeks snatched Medea and Paris evened the score by taking Helen, but the Greeks then escalated the conflict by destroying Troy. Herodotus comments: "That's what the Persians and the Phoenicians say; I have no intention of saying that these things happened one way or another. Instead I will indicate the man who I myself know began unjust acts against the Greeks ... ," Croesus, king of Lydia (1.5).

When I assign this passage and ask students, "What does Herodotus say was the origin of the conflict between the Persians and the Greeks?" they almost invariably respond by saying that he thinks it was the seizure of women. In their defense, Herodotus does use half a dozen paragraphs to describe these abductions. But students don't see that the text plainly doubts these stories. Not just another instance of students' lax reading, this blindness indicates a far more profound difference between me and them, a difference about how we approach history itself.

Herodotus draws several contrasts in these opening paragraphs. We might distinguish between mythical characters (like Helen) and an actual king (like Croesus, who ruled Lydia from 560 to 546 BCE). Herodotus, however, does not explicitly contrast myth with history. But he does state an important difference in the proper subject of history: While the Persians' stories involve occasional raiding and flashing destruction, Croesus built a durable structure of power: "For the first time among the foreigners we know, this Croesus subjected some Greeks to the payment of tribute and attached other as allies ... . Before Croesus' empire, all the Greeks were free" (1.6). Empire inaugurates history.

More than just an assertion of the proper subject of history, however, Herodotus's opening offers a deep methodological claim: Doubt underpins historical knowing. He neither ratifies nor denounces others' stories (*logoi*), he predicates neither their truth nor their falsity. Instead, he repeats and questions them. Herodotus not only treats his sources with doubt—implying that one might contradict *any* story about the past, including his own—but also *begins* with doubt, and founds his claims of knowing on it. He does not oppose doubt to knowing, but presents doubting stories of the past as integral to telling them. Knowing does not banish doubt; it asserts responsibility in the face of its pervasiveness.

I share Herodotus' belief that history is essentially dubious, but my students do not, at least at first. Their understanding—if I may lump them all together and put it baldly—is that history is knowledge of facts about the past, information that might provide a leg up on *Jeopardy*. Roland Barthes diagnosed their condition with more nuance: students suffer from the "reality effect." Historical discourse, for Barthes, depends upon three things: the referent, the signified, and the sign. The referent is the thing that happened in the world. The signified is a (usually) linguistic trace of this event, what historians call a "source." The sign, finally, is the historian's text. For Barthes, an event (the referent) is not something that meaningfully exists outside of and prior to language; instead, historians create the event when they posit it (through their language) as an external ground for the source (the signified). Barthes argues that historians then make a second move: they elide the source (the signified) so that they claim that their narratives (the signs) merely represent the events (the referents).

I think it would be unfair to accuse most contemporary historians of a naïve complicity with this "reality effect" in their historical practice, since most historians foreground the complexities of their evidence and the challenges of using it. But Barthes's term may have more purchase as a description of what happens in classrooms (physical or virtual). When students seek knowledge, we give them lectures, when they expect facts, we assign textbooks, and when they crave certainty, we preside as authorities.

I prefer a pedagogy that more closely conforms to my writing: beginning with, emphasizing, and never forgetting doubt. (I began teaching at small, liberal arts colleges, where I learned to teach from students with different expectations than those I now confound at a large, public university.) Without the anchor of the textbook, the itinerary of the lectures, and the authority of the captain (insofar as a man in a tie can duck that role), challenged not to learn information but to make inferences from evidence, students drift, explore, create—not an easy task, as the man in the tie relentlessly heckles them: "Where do you see evidence for that in the text?" Doubt dogs them.

I was explaining this recently to my colleague Bill Beazley, who noted that it takes boldness, even courage, to make a positive claim about the past. This is Herodotus's boldness: "I will indicate the man who I myself know began unjust acts against the Greeks." Herodotus here is not making an assertion imperiously. Quite the contrary, by inserting himself he is taking responsibility for knowing in the face of doubt, he is making himself an accountable historian. At the big bang of history as a discipline and a genre, in the very first words of the oldest history in the Western tradition, the first created particles were not facts about the past, but the historian and his curiosity: "This is the display of the inquiry of Herodotus of Halicarnassus ... ." This is the instant when inquiry, *historie*, became history.

Doubt underpins knowing by multiplying ignorance and fostering curiosity.

> I heard much else in Memphis when I went to the priests of Hephaistos for their stories. In fact because of this I detoured to Thebes and Heliopolis. I wanted to know if they would agree with the stories I heard in Memphis, and the people in Heliopolis are said to know more stories than other Egyptians (2.3).

Someone's story is not the end of inquiry, but the beginning.

Students respond to Herodotus's history with various degrees of incredulousness, as have professional historians. Far from failing to present a sufficiently scientific or objective history, however, Herodotus confounds commonplace ideas about how to write and read history. The readers' wariness is not a failure but an essential aspect of inquiry. Herodotus, it seems to me, is not primarily concerned with truth. Not with the discourse of *aletheia* (truth, something his characters talk about more than he does in his own voice), nor fundamentally with the correspondence of a story to what actually happened.

> The Carthaginians say that nearby lies an island named Kyrauis ... . [They say that] there's a marsh on it from which young women of the place use bird feathers smeared with pitch to bring up gold dust from the mud. I don't know whether this is true; I'm just writing down what they said. But anything is possible since I myself have seen also in Zakynthos tar being

drawn up out of the water of a lake. [Herodotus now describes this practice and the lake that apparently empties into the sea through a subterranean river.] If this is so, even what's reported about the island lying near Libya resembles truth (4.195).

Instead of focusing on truth, working to achieve the "reality effect," Herodotus focuses on the knowing subject: the relationship of the inquirer to others' stories and of the storyteller to his own. In such a text even the occasional assertion that "it is as it was" (to quote what the Pope may or may not have said about Mel Gibson's movie about the Passion) raises doubts, not only because it makes explicit the doubt it's responding to, but also because it sharpens the responsibility of the teller. Generally, Herodotus presents himself not as a truthful authority but as an accountable knower.

At the University of Arizona, I helped develop and routinely teach an introductory course for history majors, one that focuses on basic concepts and skills. During that course, I challenge students to consider the value of newspapers as sources by having them read the article by Judith Miller and Michael Gordon, "US says Hussein intensifies quest for A-bomb parts," which appeared on the front page of the Sunday *New York Times* on September 8, 2002. You may recall this as one of the most notable instances of Miller's infamous reporting: Iraq had attempted to get aluminum tubes, the article claimed, to use in centrifuges to enrich uranium for nuclear bombs. But the long article (over 3,400 words) ranged broadly, describing not only Iraq's past nuclear program, but Saddam Hussein's previous development and use of chemical and biological weapons. It was all deeply portentous, even the *absence* of evidence: "The first sign of a 'smoking gun,' they [hard-liners] argue, may be a mushroom cloud."

Consider how context determines meaning. On the article's continuation page sit two unsettling but gratuitous photographs: one of Iraq's Revolutionary Command Council, a line of glowering Saddam clones saluting; the other an aerial view of an isolated industrial plant in Iraq, billowing dark smoke. Or turn back to the first page. In the Sunday paper closest to the first anniversary of the attacks of September 11, every front-page article concerned either those attacks or the threatened war on Iraq. Two of the articles—a report on public opinion on the war on terror and an interview with Secretary of State Colin Powell—at least registered the possibility of dissent on the question of whether the United States should attack Iraq. But that possibility was framed within a larger story that already implicitly linked the al-Qaida attacks with Iraq—not just by those who wanted war, but by the editors of the *New York Times*. (My students alerted me to these important contexts. I had downloaded a text-only version of Miller's article, but some of them had used different databases, and examined a copy of the whole front page. The choice of database, it turns out, matters.)

Although the impression left by the article was entirely misleading—Iraq neither possessed nor was it developing any of these weapons—Miller and Gordon scrupulously hedged every positive assertion by attributing it to a source (usually anonymous). In reporting the *logoi* of others, their article looks a little like Herodotus's history.

> Whether Xerxes sent a herald to Argos who said these things and whether the Argive ambassadors went up to Susa and offered Artaxerxes an alliance, I cannot precisely say, nor do I offer an opinion except what the Argives themselves say … . I must tell what was said, but I'm not required to believe it all—and this is my rule for the rest of this work (*logos*) (7.152).

But in precisely this similarity the radical difference emerges: by introducing himself explicitly as the subject who both records the stories of others and offers one of his own, Herodotus makes doubt and accountability—not authority—the essential practices of knowing.

Readers are always complicit in an author's cons. When Joan Didion admitted that "writers are always selling somebody out," she was talking about her sources, but she could have been (and perhaps was) referring to her readers as well. In teaching, we train readers. We can have them read textbooks and attend lectures—selling them out to the next trickster with a concocted war—or we can cultivate their doubt, their ignorance, their curiosity.

The Shakespeare Teacher: Shakespeare's Globe and the Prisoner's World

Carol Symes

"I have been studying," says Shakespeare's imprisoned king, "how I may compare / This prison where I live unto the world."[1] The comparison is not so difficult after all, because Richard II is not really in solitary confinement: he's talking to that microcosm of humanity contained in William Shakespeare's theatre, The Globe. Time and again, Shakespeare's characters suffer imprisonment or exile; time and again, his actors compare "this cockpit," and the world itself, to a prison.[2] Like all of the new playhouses constructed in the late 16th century, the Globe was a confined space. But it was more liberating than the other contemporaneous enclosures that were forcing rural laborers off once-common land, bringing thousands of impoverished vagabonds to London. This newly criminalized underclass would supply some of the performers who staffed the licensed theatres of Southwark's "red light" district, and it would also produce the purveyors and consumers of less respectable entertainments: bear-baiting, cock-fighting, prostitution. On stage, actors played kings and queens; out in the real world, they were more likely to have seen the inside of a dungeon than a royal court. Many audience members would have recognized themselves as those "guilty creatures sitting at play" who (according to Hamlet) "Have by the very cunning of the scene / Been struck so to the soul that presently / They have proclaimed their malefactions."[3]

These verses were greeted by some sharp intakes of breath when recited by the actor playing Hamlet in a scene staged at the Danville Correctional Center (Danville, Illinois) in January 2012. He was a convicted felon, as were many members of the audience—their crimes largely the same as those enumerated by Henry V in another scene. "Some, peradventure, have on them the guilt of premeditated and contrived murder; some, of beguiling virgins with the broken seals of perjury [or, put another way, rape and aggravated sexual assault]; some ... have gored the gentle bosom of peace with pillage and robbery."[4] As he spoke, the inmate playing Henry pointed to particular men in the room. Shakespeare's original Henry may have done the same, according to the interactive conventions of the Elizabethan playhouse.

Experienced Shakespearean actors know that they have to "cast the audience," to involve spectators in the action and thereby make them complicit in the villains' plots or the lovers' secret vows. But when things go terribly wrong for Othello and Desdemona, why does no one speak up and expose Iago's perfidy? Or cry out, as the reluctant Second Murderer does in Richard III—"Look behind you, my lord!"—in a failed attempt to save the Duke of Clarence from his more ruthless partner?[5] Today's theatre audience is trained to be silent. In Shakespeare's theatre, as in the makeshift theatre of this medium-maximum security prison, the audience reacted in more lively ways. Yet even they wouldn't actively intervene, perhaps because being an informant carries, in prison, a stigma comparable to that of being gay. It therefore took considerable daring for the actors who played Bassanio and Antonio (in a scene from *The Merchant of Venice*) to bring out the homoerotic undertones of that relationship; their comic skill elicited cathartic laughter. Richard III's bumbling hit men got a lot of laughs, too, especially when one of them lamented that his conscience "made me once restore a purse of gold that, *by chance*, I had ... found."[6]

After the first performance, we were no longer allowed to show the murder of Clarence on stage, because the wardens judged this to be inappropriate. So might some choice bit of scripted business have been censored on the Elizabethan stage: one reason why Shakespeare and his contemporaries scripted only words, not actions. It was also why they let their "clowns speak more than is set down for them"—because impromptu business is harder to control.[7] Yet even a "licensed" fool could find himself stepping beyond the bounds. In retrospect, I realize how risky it was to let our Clown mimic the conventions of Shakespeare's fools by singing a popular song that resonated with his audience, rather than the song preserved in the script of *Hamlet*.

> Mama, just killed a man:
> Put a gun against his head,
> Pulled my trigger, now he's dead.
> Mama, life had just begun,
> But now I've gone and thrown it all away.[8]

So crooned our gravedigger, as he tossed imaginary clods of dirt out of an imaginary hole—the earbuds of his MP3 player making him oblivious to Hamlet's approach. In fact, what almost shut us down was my naïve decision to use common objects from the prison as props, thinking that the prohibition of anything overtly theatrical applied only to things brought in from "outside." That prohibition turned out to encompass rubber balls from the gym that we used as skulls, as well as the crown I'd made out of a piece of scissored paper and some tape. Apparently, I had managed in a few minutes to manufacture an inflammatory object—a symbol of one of the prison's gangs.

In Shakespeare's world, an acting company could be fined or imprisoned for flouting the laws, even unknowingly. In the world of prison, the penalty would be worse: the closing of theatre itself, and maybe weeks in "the hole" for members of my cast. It could also mean my permanent exile from the place that had become, in five fleeting months, oddly beloved and terribly moving: my creative refuge and my research site, the place where cheerful (jeering?) voices greeted me as I crossed the windy prison yard. "Hey, Shakespeare teacher!"

I am not, officially, a Shakespeare teacher. I'm an historian who has studied the intersection of theatre and public life in medieval Europe, and the chancy processes that govern the ways that information about performed activity is transmitted in writing (then and now). But Shakespeare's language, characters, and worldviews have shaped my existence since I saw my first play, *As You Like It*, at the age of seven. For the next 30 years, I seized every opportunity to read, discuss, watch, teach, or act in Shakespeare's plays. I eventually trained as an actress, at the Bristol Old Vic Theatre School in England, and I worked in theatre professionally while working toward the PhD, which I earned in the same year as my Equity card. But then I left a flexible teaching position at Bennington College and the northeastern theatres that had learned to tolerate my academic day job. I moved to the University of Illinois, and set about the task of getting tenure and turning myself into a serious scholar. And while I continued to work Shakespeare into every crevice that could contain a quotation, a part of me was slowly starving away. I began to conceptualize a project that would allow me to engage with Shakespeare again, through a sort of labor history of the entertainers who preceded him: their status, training, and social roles. And someday, I thought, I'd find a way to perform Shakespeare again.

Then, in spring 2011, I went to hear some of my colleagues talk about teaching *pro bono* for the Education Justice Project (EJP). Founded in 2006 by a small group of Illinois faculty and graduate students, it now offers several courses each semester at the overcrowded prison in nearby Danville. I learned that EJP's students, mostly African American, have already earned associate's degrees and have somehow sustained a high degree of ambition despite decades of incarceration; many have been imprisoned since they were teenagers, usually for murder and other gang- or drug-related crimes. As I listened to the incandescent testimony of the faculty who had taught these eager, eloquent men—in courses on the Holocaust and cultural memory, the history of madness, classical philosophy, biology, landscape architecture—I thought about the short essay that one of the students had contributed to an EJP newsletter, explaining that he and his classmates "encourage[d] one another to think outside the box, meaning the mentally confined space formed in the course of our daily mundane activities."[9] I realized that I was hearing a paraphrase of some familiar lines.

> Thus play I, in one person, many people—
> And none contented. Sometimes I am a king
> Then treasons make me wish myself a beggar
> And so I am. Then crushing penury
> Persuades me I was better when a king.
> Then am I king'd again, and by and by
> Think that I am unking'd by Bolingbroke
> And straight am nothing. But what e'er I be
> Nor I nor any man but that man is
> With nothing shall be pleased till he be eased
> With being nothing.[10]

Within his cell, Richard II accomplished what the actors of Shakespeare's company did within the confines of The Globe, and what the students of EJP were clearly doing, too: experimenting with roles different than those forced upon them by circumstance, thinking beyond their narrow existence. In the face of constant humiliation, the threat of solitary confinement, the torpor of hopelessness, their intelligence, perseverance, and empathy enabled them to create new identities. I couldn't imagine anything that would nourish them more, or give them better tools, than Shakespeare's plays. I wanted to show them how their world intersected with Shakespeare's: with The Globe, with the world of late 16th-century England, with the often exotic (but always local) worlds of the plays themselves.

What I couldn't anticipate was the effect of "Shakespeare's Worlds" on my understanding of the plays and their historical milieu, and on my research into the relationship between theatre's textual residue and the conditions that shape performance. Far from being the last place that one should experience

Shakespeare, the prison turned out to be a laboratory for the purest kind of theatre—stripped down to its elements and as nakedly powerful as Lear on the heath. I am not the first person to notice this; I didn't know, then, that Shakespeare's plays flourish in a number of prisons all over the world.[11] Indeed, I had never given much thought to the carceral landscape of Shakespeare's London and the ways that the language, metaphors, and reality of imprisonment would have resonated with his actors and audiences. Most immediately, I did not expect my students to want to engage in performance—beyond the requirement (stipulated in the syllabus) that they memorize and present a speech or scene from one of the six plays we studied: *Richard III*, *The Merchant of Venice*, *Julius Cæsar*, *Henry V*, *Hamlet*, and *Othello*. They hadn't expected to perform, either. Most didn't want to be in the class at all. Of the 15 who enrolled, 10 were extremely suspicious; only a few had ever read a play or seen one performed, and these experiences were usually negative. One student dropped the class after the first day. But on the other end of the spectrum was a student who was already a seasoned actor. (A theatre major in college before coming to Danville, his favorite role was Bottom in *A Midsummer Night's Dream*.) A few inmates were aspiring poets, and they responded with mingled interest and disbelief when I compared Shakespeare to their favorite rap artists and the screenwriters of action movies and crime dramas on TV.

What really galvanized the class was the unexpected familiarity of the first play we read, *Richard III*, and its world of casual crime and cyclical violence. "We all know guys like that," they told me. Unlike today's classical actors, or the audiences drawn to allegedly élite cultural artifacts, my students know firsthand the manipulations, betrayals, inequities, and vengeful caprice experienced by Shakespeare's contemporaries. In prison, they learn to negotiate the minefield of an authoritarian regime not so different from Elizabethan England. In every class, they would illuminate some dramatic situation that I had failed to appreciate or explain the enigmatic motives of a character that I had long misinterpreted. For example, when Marc Antony sends a slave to greet Cæsar's assassins with flattering words,[12] I called him a coward. Not so, my students insisted: Antony wouldn't risk losing face by going himself; he'd want to assess the situation and play for time until he'd assembled sufficient backup and a plan of action. They penetrated the veneer of Shakespeare's Plutarch and deep into the play's contests of power and masculinity, particularly in the confrontation between Brutus and Cassius before Philippi, which we eventually staged as a confrontation between two leaders of a riven gang.[13] Tapping into their shared knowledge of group dynamics, the famous scene between Antony and the Roman crowd became electrifying and dangerous, a blend of self-serving demagoguery, opportunism, and sincere grief.

I hadn't planned to direct a play in a prison, or to alter my own research trajectory. But that is what happened. Six weeks into the class, my students were vying with one another for time "on stage," bravely getting up to collapse the boundaries between Shakespeare's worlds and their own, and bringing their own rich insights to these enactments. We decided to try what had been inconceivable at the beginning: to construct our own play, so that we could share Shakespeare with others in the prison who thought he had nothing to say to them. We chose a number of scenes and wove them into a new five-act drama that dealt with the power of persuasion, the lure of violence, the tragedy of revenge, and the now obvious relationships between the theatre and the prison. It was called *Our Play*, and it opened with an ensemble performance of *Henry V*'s opening Chorus ("Who Prologue-like your humble patience pray / Gently to hear, kindly to judge, *our play*").[14] It closed with Hamlet's encounter with Rosencrantz and Guildenstern ("Denmark's a prison") and the entry of "the best actors in the world": my students.[15] Along the way, it anatomized the murder of Cæsar, Iago's manipulation of Othello, Shylock's enraged response to generations of bigotry and exclusion, a Ghost's revelation of his own damnation ("sent to my account / With all my imperfections on my head. / O horrible, O horrible, most horrible!"[16]), a king's realization that he cannot escape eternal judgment (even though "In the corrupted currents of this world / Offence's gilded hand may shove by justice"[17]), and many other scenes that took on fresh, vibrant meanings in this setting.

I make no claims for the "authenticity" of this approach. But I do claim that the awkward logistics governing our performance were analogous to those that constrained Shakespeare's actors. My students too had to carve out a space for free speech, protest, civility, and artistry through constant management of imperious and often capricious institutional demands. They too brought varying talents and degrees of education to the realization of roles. They too learned their lines in isolation from one another, using handmade cue scripts, with minimal rehearsal time. They too adjusted constantly to the distractions of their environment during performance, in a minimally equipped space with no special effects, no special lighting, and no place to hide from the spectators' searching gaze. Most strikingly, they too carried little historical baggage to the performance: no stifling consciousness of iconic performances to which they must adhere, or attempt to resist. And like Shakespeare's company, my students performed for people who had never heard these lines spoken before, and who responded with intense enjoyment, surprise, and recognition of themselves in the mirror of the play.

How might we begin to reinterpret the workings of Shakespeare's plays in light of these discoveries? How might my students' insights prompt new research on the playhouses and the prisons of Shakespeare's London, and the people who frequented both? These are questions I intend to explore in the future. For now, I already see important feedback loops forming. The courage it took these men (self-described "tough guys") to inhabit these plays, while putting intimate aspects of themselves on display, has given them all a new kind of confidence. All of them were cast (or cast themselves) in roles that required a working-through of long-buried memories or unacknowledged pain; and many found it possible to empathize deeply with characters they would once have dismissed as wholly different from themselves. Moreover, mounting *Our Play* required them to work as a team (rarely encouraged in prison), and a team not determined by racial divisions or gang affiliations. This daunting challenge, and its ultimate success, has fostered the trust and camaraderie that results from accomplishing something difficult and collaborative—an experience many were probably seeking, in vain, back in the days when they first joined a gang. My students have become, in their own favorite phrase, the "band of brothers" ("We few, we happy few").[18] And they are hungry to share what they've learned with a widening circle: other students in the Education Justice Project, five of whom have since joined our acting troupe; the larger prison population, at first hostile or indifferent to the performance of Shakespeare but now curious, even enthusiastic; family members and friends on the outside, who routinely listen to speeches recited over the phone and who are now able to watch a video of *Our Play* online; and, perhaps most significantly, kids back in their old neighborhoods, in the projects, on Chicago's South Side. They want to be Shakespeare teachers.

Acknowledgement

This essay is dedicated to the students of "Shakespeare's Worlds" and the actors of *Our Play*, produced by the Education Justice Project and staged at Danville Correctional Center in January of 2012: Abdul Akram, George Bledsoe, Antyon (Mupha) Brown, Gregory A. Donatelli, Joseph Findlay, Robert Garite, James Green, Johnny Page, Kemuyah Ben Rakemeyahu, Chad Rand, Emmett Sanders, Samuel Santiago, Anthony Skaug, and Shaun Wilkes. Thanks are due to Wardens Keith Anglin and Victor Calloway for making this production possible. It can viewed online at http://vimeo.com/45168866. The Band of Brothers perfomed its first full-length play, *The Tempest*, in April of 2013.

Notes

1. William Shakespeare, *Richard III*, 5.5.1-2. All citations are from *The Norton Shakespeare, Based on the Oxford Edition*, 2d ed., ed. Stephen Greenblatt et al. (New York, 2008).

2. *Henry V*, prologue, 11.

3. *Hamlet*, 2.2.566–569.

4. *Henry V*, 5.1.151–155.

5. *Richard III*, 2.1.256.

6. *Richard III*, 1.5.132 (this was the actor's own line reading).

7. Of course, Hamlet—that controlling, amateur playwright, says the opposite: "Let not your clowns speak more than is set down for them" (*Hamlet*, 3.2.34–35).

8. Freddy Mercury and Queen, "Bohemian Rhapsody," from *A Night at the Opera* (1975).

9. Andra D. Slater, "Staying outside of the Box," *Education Justice Project Newsletter* 9 (Spring 2010): 1.

10. *Richard II*, V.v, vv. 31–41.

11. One of these, Shakespeare Behind Bars, originated at the Luther Luckett Correctional Complex in LaGrange, Kentucky; it is the subject of an award-winning documentary of that name by Hank Rogerson (2005). Another, Prison Performing Arts, serves multiple constituencies in the St. Louis area. Its production of *Hamlet*'s Act V was featured on National Public Radio's *This American Life* (Episode 218, on August 9, 2002). On the missions and effects of such programs, see Amy Scott-Douglas, *Shakespeare Inside: The Bard Behind Bars* (London and New York, 2007); and Jonathan Shailor, *Performing New Lives: Prison Theatre* (London and Philadelphia, 2011).

12. *Julius Cæsar* 3.1.123–138.

13. *Julius Cæsar* 4.2.

14. *Henry V*, prologue, 33–34.

15. *Hamlet*, 2.2, 239 and 379.

16. *Hamlet*, 1.5.78–80.

17. *Hamlet*, 3.3.57–58.

18. *Henry V*, 4.3.60.

Global India and the Divergent Temporalities of South Asia

Shefali Chandra

Three months after I started my first tenure-track job, the United States invaded Iraq. It was 2003, and the classroom was a space of important political debate. Even the most jaded back-bencher in my large survey class came to acknowledge that history mattered, that an understanding of colonialism and the insights of postcolonial theory were essential tools for understanding the contemporary world. Of course, the learning curve was steep, most especially for me. Halfway into a semester teaching the South Asia History Survey, I was still reminding students that "South Asia" was not the same as South *East* Asia: the collective unconscious of colonial history echoed eerily through the class. After seven weeks on the history of British colonialism, we turned to the themes of decolonization and the Cold War. As we talked about the political contours of the area, one student raised his hand to ask why "don't India, China, or Great Britain invade Nepal and Bhutan?" Turning his question back to the class only dumbfounded me further. Every aspect of my lectures over the past weeks had sprung from a rejection of imperialism, a critique of the calculations of global capitalism. Now, not one student grappled with the ethics of larger nation-states invading smaller ones—perhaps an inevitable lapse for students barely teenagers at the start of the "War on Terror." Mostly, my students provided instrumentalist reasoning: perhaps Bhutan and Nepal did not have the kind of resources that India possessed in the 18th century; perhaps their geographical location (surrounded by mountains rather than oceans) made them difficult to access. Do larger countries see a need to take over smaller ones in this age of neocolonial and multinational capital?

Hawkishness and historical analyses conjoined, the class had framed an astute understanding of the political reality of globalization and the South Asian subcontinent. The fact that India was the only South Asian country named as a potential aggressor was crucial. A few years later, teaching a version of the same survey at a private research university with a very selective undergraduate population, I was surprised to hear variants on the same theme: India as superpower. Successive groups of students used India, South Asia, and South *East* Asia interchangeably; when pushed to disaggregate, they talked about the South Asian countries as though they existed to provide resources for the material needs of India. For group projects in which they devised their own topics, students invariably presented on Bollywood, Indian food, nonviolence, and Indian classical dance. When pushed to present on the other South Asian countries, they composed projects on "terrorism," "natural disaster alleviation," and "human rights for homosexuals."

The affinity with India, the anticipation of its regional hegemony, and an investment in its seemingly durable cultural identity came together with their interest in de-linking the region into two cultural zones. "India" the core; "South Asia" the cultural and economic periphery, lying firmly in the temporal and cultural shadow of that core. Most of my students were children of Indian white-collar workers who had settled in the United-States after 1965. They were products of the class-selective immigration policies that defined the hyper-specialized industries of medicine, information technology, and increasingly, higher education in the United States.[1] But quite a few of my students were Pakistani, Sri-Lankan, and Bangladeshi, and even they seemed disposed to celebrate India while placing other South Asian countries in its shadow. The non-South Asian students were more inclined still to celebrate India alone.

As a cultural studies project, the task seemed intriguing: how could I account for process and historicize the investment in and desire for Indian global and regional hegemony? At the same time, as an area-based scholar, my inclination was to resist national frames of understanding while wresting all South Asian countries from the shadow of India and US-centered geopolitics.[2] As a feminist and postcolonial scholar, I was interested in unpacking narratives of origin—the linear and presentist teleologies that would craft "India" as an already emergent whole. My classroom interactions were pushing me beyond an established chronology of the region whereby "India" was the only entity granted historical traction, the students were demanding a deeper assessment of decolonization whereby every

South Asian country appeared merely a limb, severed from the organic continuity of "India." The solution, for me, emerged from the political-economic connections between postcolonial state formation, the Cold War, and South Asian immigration. For all the advances made by postcolonial literary and cultural studies, scholarship on the actual postcolonial period remained in the hands of political scientists and a handful of anthropologists. Area Studies was itself guilty: a proliferation of monographs claiming to study "South Asia" in actuality focused on India. We called ourselves South Asianists, but with some very notable exceptions, we were Indianists. Despite that, a historical understanding of the transnational desire for India, one that took seriously the politics of the postcolonial world and of globalization, and that unpacked the role of India in cohering South Asia and US imperialism, remained elusive.

In response, I framed two undergraduate classes—one an interactive lecture-discussion introductory course, the other a selective upper-level research-intensive seminar—on the theme of "Indian globalization." Both courses rely on student research; I provide interdisciplinary theoretical tools from history, postcolonial studies, cultural studies, feminist theory, and Asian American studies. I organize the class not around the historical story of the Indian nation, but work instead to treat 'India' as a cultural form itself and understand transmission of the *concept* of India: how it circulates, in whose hands, and toward what ends. Three segments overlap. For the first part, we work on the historicity of India, though not through the usual turning points that structure my survey class. Rather than the markers of Vasco Da Gama's voyage, the Battle of Plassey, Lord Bentinck's ban on sati, the 1857 uprising, the inauguration of the Indian National Congress, etc., we mull over when and why the concept of "India" entered wider debates on transnational interconnections: whether in William Jones's linguistic theories, Karl Marx's writings on imperialism, spiritual treatises from the Theosophists, American Romanticism, Martha Nussbaum on feminism, or Taslima Nasreen on freedom. What did "India" mean from the eighteenth century to the present? This section provides the historical spine for what follows. The next and overlapping component of the course examines the material sites on which the knowledge of India has been produced and circulated: economics, history, feminism, fiction, self-help studies, film, the Internet. We turn last to South Asia: what are the essential identities that the Indian state and its literati have developed for its neighbors (Islamic, terroristic, underdeveloped, open-for-business)? What are the social categories that materialize, and cohere, South Asian countries? And how in turn can we learn about South Asian countries stripped of those associations?

Even as I pull together my primary sources and compose my lectures, I imagine generations of historians rolling their eyes at my "discursive" studies. My own experience suggests that this is one way to bridge area studies with world history. Locating the movement of "goods, peoples, and ideas" alongside 300 years of the transnational formulation of "India," as these courses do, brings history into conversation with cultural studies, helping us to appreciate a range of sources less for their content than their historical positioning. Alongside world history, cultural studies, and literary postcolonial studies, the theoretical edifice for these courses draws from materialist feminist studies: I anchor the classes through an understanding of the political economy of desire.[3] Finally, queer studies' emphasis on the trained fabrication of gender spills over into our appreciation for the performativity of "India"—how it becomes materialized through specific practices such as food, fashion, or fiction, all attuned to the desires of a class-specific transnational audience.

The most exciting aspect of these courses for me has been the role of student research. Small seminars are of course tailor-made for research, but my happiest discovery has been that of incorporating student research into plans for a future, large lecture course. I intersperse group projects throughout the semester. Students give presentations on "When Americans Discovered Yoga," "The English Language in Hindi Cinema," "Tata Cars in South Africa," "Saving Bangladeshi Women from Fatwas," "Gestational Outsourcing," and "Pipelines and Peripheries." Here it is my Facebook-inhabiting, tech-savvy undergraduates who trawl the Internet, work with the university's area librarian, imagine one another as the audience, and collectively cull the data on Indian globalization.

The archive and narrative for Indian globalization is not to be found in conventional, state-controlled depositories or in the textbooks under circulation. There is much to be gleaned from the Internet, and undergraduates make the best research assistants. More importantly, as they shape their discoveries to the format of the group presentation, they produce archives that privilege their peers as their intended audience. The temporality of knowledge and the reality of the digital divide can thus be discussed at the very moment of their formulation; the conceit and power of the American classroom provides the ground for further reflection on the transnational desires of imperial power.

Trained as a historian of South Asia, my dissertation research entailed a careful study of the history of Indian education over the colonial, 19th, and first half of the 20th century. But in the classroom (to return to the question that unites the essays in this collection), alongside South Asia courses, I teach on sexuality, empire, and world history. Increasingly, the post 9/11 environment alongside the rise of the Internet has produced a new kind of interest in, and understanding of, South Asia. Postcolonial theory, which analyses the vertical relationship between metropolitan interests and the colonies, has been invigorated by more recent studies on the lateral connectivities of the past 50 years.[4] This major shift in the organization of capital and labor has been accompanied by innovative cultural imaginaries, themselves moored to new associative forms like nongovernmental organizations, national-religious corporations, and social networking sites. Shifting imperial formations, the neo-colonial native informant,[5] the conditions of work and migration,[6] and relating change over time to the transformation in imperial power over the past 300 years, are all subjects that require our sustained attention. Critical feminist studies have helped to historicize the desire for seemingly transhistorical and transnational cultural categories, such as "woman." Similarly, my task here is to unpack the seeming coherence of "India" alongside the movement of Indian financial and cultural capital, to alert us to the living logic of contemporary imperialism.

In these fresh and significant ways, my students have pushed my research questions and not merely my classroom lectures. As I bring cultural studies together with queer theory and area/ethnic studies, I nevertheless face major gaps in my conceptual apparatus. My humanities-based training cannot guide me through the terrain of macroeconomic terminology; I struggle with vulgar conjunctures between political economy and culture. Research time, research funds, and the existence of interdisciplinary units will be essential to reaching for new topics and methodologies, as will be the ability to bring faculty and students into conversation across disciplines and academic settings. Conferences, language teaching, and research clusters must frame intellectual enquiry. No question, however pertinent, can be sustained merely by a captive audience of agreeable undergraduates.

In unpacking the myth of globalization, it is important to see how our desire for apparently benign cultural forms sanctions the existence of a uniform system of exchange for the entire world. How does our investment in a durable Indian culture reflect on the reality of the Indo-US relationship,[7] and further, how does that relationship condone US financial- and military-based "democracy"? My courses on Indian globalization—on the collective interest in making the world safe for US-centered corporate capital—have confirmed for me the need for interdisciplinary theoretical tools, new archives, and new theories on empire.[8] I recognize that a course on Indian regional power and globalization stands the risk of merely augmenting the very desire for India that I have set out to unravel. But in the process of historicizing the historic invocation of India—the manner by which India entered into the Cold War, the presence and power of diasporic Indians, the wide purchase of an essential Indian culture, the relationship between India and the US during the wars in Afghanistan, Iraq, and Pakistan, the new land grabs by India in African nations, the rise of outsourcing facilities and the cultish regard for "Bollywood," Islamophobia, the rise of China, India's subimperial power in the region—in all these areas and more we see important evidence on the way that imperialism operates today. Traditional disciplines are inadequate to this imperial moment, to the historical narrative that threatens to re-center "India" via an overdetermination on the "national" and a disregard for the production of meaning. Bringing in feminist theory and ethnic and cultural studies allows for a robust understanding of the totalizing fantasies of globalization and the disparate contingencies of contemporary imperialism.

Notes

1. Vijay Prashad, *The Karma of Brown Folk* (Minneapolis: University of Minnesota Press, 2000); Sunaina Maira, *Desis in the House: Indian American Youth Culture in NYC* (Philadelphia: Temple University Press, 2002).

2. David Ludden, "Area Studies in the Age of Globalization," *Frontiers: The Interdisciplinary Journal of Study Abroad* (Winter 2000): 1–22.

3. Lisa Rofel, *Desiring China: Experiments in Neoliberalism, Sexuality, and Public Culture* (Durham, NC: Duke University Press, 2007).

4. Michael Hardt and Antonio Negri, *Empire* (Cambridge, MA: Harvard University Press, 2000).

5. Antoinette Burton, *The Postcolonial Careers of Santa Rama Rau* (Durham, NC: Duke University Press, 2007).

6. Michele Ruth Gamburd, *The Kitchen Spoon's Handle: Transnationalism and Sri-Lanka's Migrant Housemaids* (New York: Cornell University Press, 2000); Dina Siddiqi, "Miracle Worker or Womanmachine? Tracking (Trans) National Realities in Bangladeshi Factories," *Economic and Political Weekly* (May 27, 2000): 11–17; Jayati Ghosh, *Never Done and Poorly Paid: Women's Work in Globalizing India* (New Delhi: Women Unlimited, 2009).

7. Saadia Toor, "IndoChic: The Cultural Politics of Consumption in Post-Liberalization India," *SOAS Literary Review* 2 (July 2000): 1–36.

8. Gayatri Spivak, *Death of a Discipline* (New York: Columbia University Press, 2003).

Teaching our Process: How Research Shapes My Teaching

Laura E. Nym Mayhall

Coming of age in the postmodern academy (when even historians read Derrida), there were times when I despaired of sharing the work of my colleagues with undergraduates. Too much translation was required. A turning point in my own development as a teacher came in a course on European cultural history I taught at Millsaps College in the mid-1990s. Eight students, none of whom had any background in cultural history, met twice weekly to discuss readings. The key to the course's success came with my realization that the students needed help in figuring out how to process their reading *while* doing it, and an environment in which they felt safe to make mistakes while working through their understanding of the material. My solution to both issues was to assign a reading journal, which then served as the primary graded work for the course. Every assigned reading was accompanied by questions for consideration in writing; I collected journals every so often and read through them, commenting in the margins. I had taken the idea for the journal from something I'd read about teaching; only while engaged in the course did I realize that my own research habits included writing-while-reading as a means of understanding. From this course, I further developed the habit of building my classes around the *process* of learning, which meant not only articulating my goals to the students explicitly, but also helping them to negotiate the sometimes painful practice of coming to terms with their own habits of work and ways of thinking.

In an ironic twist, the realization that my own research process could shape my pedagogical practice turned out to be harder to implement in a research institution than it had at a liberal arts college. When I began teaching at the Catholic University of America a few years later, I discovered that the institutional culture of a research university emphasized process far less than it did content, drawing a brighter line between the two than had my earlier experience. Most surprisingly, I found that students resisted my approach far more than did my colleagues. But I continue to refuse posing "process" and "content" in purely dichotomous terms. Content is acquired *through* process, but it requires an active method on the students' part. It requires also a self-conscious approach on the part of the instructor. The research we do for our own articles and books does not require us to memorize or "be exposed to" massive amounts of information. Our teaching should not assume that our "coverage," or the mere presentation of material, means that students have engaged in the *activity* of making that new material their own. Two points follow from this observation: one, that the lecture as a mode of presentation should be used self-consciously, not reflexively; and two, that the distance between our "own work" (our research) and our teaching is less than the oppositional pairing of "teaching and research" suggests.

I will say relatively little here about the first of these points, except to note that research in a number of fields increasingly indicates that students learn less from passively listening to lectures than they do from active engagement with course material. The scholarship on this question is large and growing; an especially cogent discussion of it is found in Ken Bain's 2004 book, *What the Best College Teachers Do*, that argues, in support of lecturing: "good explanations come from people who realize that learners must construct knowledge rather than simply absorb it."[1] This first point is connected to the second in that both see learning, like research, as an active process—one in which *the struggle to understand* defines the success of the enterprise. Or to put it another way: a more active process of acquiring knowledge results in a stronger hold on that knowledge.

But how does one convey to students the importance of the struggle for understanding? The largest class I teach at Catholic University is a world history survey capped at 60 students, and enrollment in our upper-division undergraduate courses is limited to 30. In these courses, my students demand of me what Virginia Woolf famously described in *A Room of One's Own* as "the first duty of a lecturer—to hand you [the student] after an hour's discourse a nugget of pure truth to wrap up between the pages of your notebooks and keep on the mantelpiece forever." Overcoming their reticence to be engaged with rather than lectured at becomes the major challenge of the course. Here, my earlier experience helped very little. Implementing writing journals in courses this large, even with the aid of teaching assistants or social media, is logistically impractical. A colleague of mine has experimented with the online blog, requiring students to make twice-weekly posts with the awareness that not only their instructor but their fellow students will follow regularly and comment on their writing. I admire my colleague's inventiveness, but my own technological acumen is less developed, and I've come to believe that a great many students still benefit from the older forms of writing and analysis that drive my own research practice: taking notes, and notes upon those notes.

Recently I've begun experimenting with a solution I first adopted to get students engaged with reading material before discussing it in class. In the first weeks of a course, I require students to complete reading/discussion worksheets rather than write formal papers. These worksheets enable them to process assigned reading prior to discussion, and they pose simple and direct questions that students frequently have trouble answering. The worksheets are presented in the following format:

Directions for Reading/Discussion Worksheets

This exercise is intended to help you with the process of reading and analyzing secondary materials. For each article read, please answer/address each of the five (5) issues below. This should result in a worksheet of five (5) paragraphs per article:

- ◆ identify the author's argument and the sources on which it is based;
- ◆ describe the author's assumptions or biases, and approach or method;
- ◆ identify the established interpretations, controversies, and literature to which the historian is responding;
- ◆ evaluate the strengths/weaknesses of the work (ask: how does the work in question contribute to our understanding of the topic? Why is it important?);
- ◆ offer your own evaluation of the article under review.

This exercise, assigned early in the semester, gives students a couple of relatively low-stakes opportunities to work through the reading by writing about it prior to our class meetings. Because the reading/discussion worksheet is afforded less weight in the final grade, students have occasions to experiment with writing as a means of sorting out their understanding with fewer adverse consequences. For some students, these initial assignments can provide early success, boosting their confidence about taking on the material. But I've also encountered problems with this approach. Some students calculate the value of the assignment and decide it isn't worth their time; they figure that an assignment worth less than ten percent of their final grade doesn't deserve their attention. More prevalent yet is the fact students sometimes simply "answer the questions," circumventing the very process in which I'm hoping they'll engage: taking notes by hand.

And here I reveal how alarmingly old-fashioned but simultaneously cutting-edge my pedagogy can be. My goal is to help students think about *how* they learn. I'm increasingly convinced, on the basis of recent research on the brain, that the act of writing itself is central to the process of mastering material. In a 2010 article in the *Wall Street Journal*, Gwendolyn Bounds reported on the findings of researchers in several fields on the relationship between writing-by-hand and deep learning. While much of her article focused on the implications of this research for elementary education, it is clear that the role writing-by-hand plays in learning is not relevant only to younger children. Bounds notes that

> Other research highlights the hand's unique relationship with the brain when it comes to composing thoughts and ideas. Virginia Berninger, a professor of educational psychology at the University of Washington, says handwriting differs from typing because it requires executing sequential strokes to form a letter, whereas keyboarding involves selecting a whole letter by touching a key. She says pictures of the brain have illustrated that sequential finger movements activated massive regions involved in thinking, language and working memory—the system for temporarily storing and managing information.[2]

Writing-by-hand (or "taking notes" as we used to call it) on reading is fast becoming a lost art. When asked, few of my students will admit to taking notes on assigned reading in this fashion, and the current obsession with metrics and rubrics contributes to the problem by requiring that we tell students precisely what is demanded of them, which feeds their belief that there is a "right" answer (the one they think we want) rather than an organic process (sometimes slow, frequently messy) through which they make sense of what they've read.

The next time I use the reading/discussion worksheet in a course, I will make two changes that I hope will address these concerns. First, I will require that students take notes on the reading by hand, and turn them in along with their worksheets. Second, I will require students to provide notes or a draft of their initial responses to the worksheet (ideally I'd require them to answer the questions on the worksheet by hand, but that may be too stringent a demand). By forcing them *literally* to write, each of these steps will give students practice using writing as a means to comprehension. In addition to stimulating the neural pathways from fingers to brain, this method also has the advantage of slowing down the process of responding to questions about the reading. Taking notes by hand requires students to make *active* choices while reading. Typing notes can devolve easily into transcription (a practice that seems to lead increasingly to unintentional forms of plagiarism), but taking notes by hand limits the amount of material one wants to reproduce and thereby provides focus during the act of reading. The reasons for these assignments will be made explicit, and I will explain that this kind of note-taking is about utilizing specific practices to attain particular ends. I suspect that some students will find this process unwieldy; I will continue to refine it. Teaching the process of learning requires self-conscious attention to the way we learn. And the research we do is built around that premise, whether we acknowledge it or not.

Notes

1. Ken Bain, *What the Best College Teachers Do* (Cambridge, MA: Harvard University Press, 2004), 126. See also http://www.npr.org/2012/01/01/144550920/physicists-seek-to-lose-the-lecture-as-teaching-tool.

2. Gwendolyn Bounds, "How Handwriting Trains the Brain: Forming Letters Is Key to Learning, Memory, Ideas," *Wall Street Journal,* October 5, 2010.

Doing "Our Own Work" as Teachers of Undergraduates

Mary Jo Maynes and Ann Waltner

"I feel so swamped since the semester started! I just can't find time for my own work!" This sentiment, or something close to it, recurs in faculty conversations and it has unsettling implications. No doubt colleagues with substantial administrative duties feel the time crunch at work most intensely. But for many, it is teaching responsibilities—undergraduate teaching responsibilities especially—that seem to be at odds with "our own work." As we face increasing pressures to teach more and larger classes, grappling creatively with this tension is becoming more urgent than ever.

Approaches to undergraduate pedagogy that keep the discipline's "ways of knowing" at their core provide a richer introduction to the field for *students*, but also offer possibilities for broadening and enriching *professors*' understandings of scholarly inquiry generally—even bringing unexpected insights to their specific fields of research. Drawing connections between undergraduate teaching and research seems relatively straightforward in the undergraduate research seminars that closely resemble graduate teaching models (themselves disappearing in a process now pushing us to rethink the pedagogy-research connection at nearly every level). But for most instructors, this is not a regular undergraduate option.

We focus here on pedagogies that can be deployed even in large undergraduate lecture classes; in particular, on constructing lectures as models of historical argumentation, and building experiments with the research process into class assignments. The small discussion sections typically appended to large lecture courses remain essential to guided close reading, analysis of scholarly works and primary sources, and teaching the critical skills our field requires. But, whether in coordination with such sections or independent of them, lecture classes can also model and teach historical ways of knowing so as to encourage discovery and research—our own as well as our students'.

Our co-taught world history classes (most recently, The Family from 10,000 BCE to the Present) use lectures to frame case studies that become the basis for comparisons students pursue through readings (of scholarly works and primary sources) and discussions (in small groups and written exercises). Many of our lectures explicitly present arguments and call attention to the sources on which those arguments are based. The question of "how we know what we know" is never far below the surface. More broadly, we have found that by encouraging students to think of lectures as arguments based on sources, and to then ask questions about those arguments (either online in sections, or during the lectures themselves), "Aha!" moments of discovery can be generated for not only the student but the instructor too. We also pause throughout the lectures to ask questions ourselves. Sometimes we are rewarded only with blank stares; other times our questions produce debate or discovery.

Let's turn to a few examples, the first from our family history course. In a lecture about encounters between family systems that are important elements of imperial rule, Waltner showed a 50-second documentary scene shot by the Lumière brothers in 1903 ("Enfants annamites ramassant des sapèques devant la pagode des dames") that depicts French women throwing coins to Indochinese children. The clip is disturbing: French women dressed in white stand inside a doorway, throwing coins at children who scramble for them in the dirt. It is a visually compelling critique of colonialism. But there are layers to the portrayal; Waltner intended to question the students (and Maynes) on the point of possible relationships to old French customs that involved throwing coins or food to children as a part of French festival life. But before the conversation got that far, a student exclaimed: "It's just like in *Martin Guerre*." Earlier in the semester, Maynes had shown a short clip from the film *The Return of Martin Guerre* in which the head of a propertied-peasant household threw coins at the young men conducting a *charivari* targeting Martin for his apparent impotence. Since Waltner had not been in class on the day the *Martin Guerre* episode was shown, she had not planned to evoke this precise parallelism. But the student's breakthrough prompted us to pursue the comparison between metropole and colony. A traditional French cultural mechanism for wealthier peasants to deal with poorer ones, and for adults to deal with unruly youth, had perhaps here been transferred to the colony, thereby allowing colonial elites to conduct a playful but symbolically charged ritual involving their young subjects. This interpretation does not blunt the critique of colonialism that the Lumière film suggests, but it raises new and nuanced questions about class, gender, and generation in cultures of colonialism. Thus, an in-class discovery made by a student illustrated a point much more vividly than we could have through lecturing alone. Indeed, the pleased astonishment with which we both responded to the unexpected insight surely made as much of an impression on our students as did anything we said in lecture.[1]

Another example emerged in a lecture class that Waltner regularly teaches on religion in China; in this case, she displayed an illustration of a consort of the Qianlong emperor (r.1735–95) dressed in Western-style armor, painted by the Jesuit court painter Giuseppe Castiglione (or one of his followers). Emperors of the Qing dynasty sometimes chose to have themselves painted in masquerade—as peasants, fishermen, or members of the European nobility. That an imperial consort was painted in European-style armor, while interesting, did not seem unusual in the context of this practice. The portrait appeared to be a gender as well as ethnic masquerade. As Waltner presented the portrait and this analysis to the class, in more or less this light, a gasp went up from the third row, and a young woman shouted: "It's Joan of Arc!" When Waltner looked at the painting again, informed now by the student's insight, it did indeed seem plausible that the painting was of the consort dressed as Joan of Arc. Subsequent digging (done mostly by the student, Meg Caines) has located a European painting of Joan bearing striking visual similarities to the portrait of the consort. Even more interesting: the original portrait was published in the mid-17th century as an illustration of a Jesuit-authored play about Joan, and was republished in a number of contexts. Thus the consort portrait's painter (also working in a Jesuit context) likely had access to the original image. As a result of this classroom discovery, Caines and Waltner are coauthoring an article that will suggest the two images may be related through world-historical processes that themselves deserve further study.

Such student responses are partly good fortune, but there are ways of structuring classes to encourage them. Creative responses can be generated and nurtured in courses whose arguments are made explicit and whose students are encouraged to engage freely and openly with scholarly sources and primary documents. This engagement can happen in lectures as well as in small-group discussions and writing assignments, in part by making clear that shout-outs from the third row are welcome additions to even the most imposing lecture halls. Assigning open-ended research projects in survey courses, while labor intensive, creates opportunities to link student questions with a wide range of historical sources and encourage them to make discoveries that can at times be quite original. The process of advising students' research in introductory classes has pushed us to rethink our use of sources or argumentation in our own research.

One example of this involves a student's work on selected aspects of family relations as reflected in a late 18th-century Prussian Law Code compared to an early 19th-century German lexicon. The main methodological point Maynes sought to convey to her advisee was that different types of historical sources can produce quite different representations of family relations in the same historical setting. But the student surprised her teacher by taking this insight a bit further, suggesting that a slightly later development (one we had read about in class: the development of German bourgeois Christmas rituals and the father's role within them) could be seen as a kind of rebellion against the authoritarian father figure as depicted in earlier Prussian family law.

Sometimes students take off on their own to explore a topic that has some particular and mysterious relevance for them. In such cases, our aim is more to support the venture than to control it. A good example of this was a student interested—for reasons that were never made entirely clear—in investigating infant baptism. After a lot of back-and-forth, Maynes helped him to find some scholarship and documents related to debates over infant baptism during the Protestant Reformation. The paper focused on theological debates between Calvin and his Anabaptist opponents, as well as on baptismal practices, and ended up astonishing Maynes in terms of its linking family relations to religion. Indeed, it became obvious to Maynes that the topic held important implications for the role of family in the process of acquiring religious status. Her marginal comments on the paper's first draft illustrate that she responded to it as a scholar critiquing a scholar's claims: "This gets more and more complex and interesting—why could only ordained ministers baptize endangered infants? What happened to them, according to Calvin, if they died without baptism?"

Teaching undergraduates has had a more direct impact on our research agendas than is perhaps generally the case because of the way our introductory-level courses have been organized: collaboratively and comparatively. Our co-teaching of world history classes has pushed us to think across field-specific historiographies. We have for a number of years engaged in joint projects that straddle teaching and research and that have resulted in a series of publications, projects that would never have been imagined without our joint teaching. We have been involved in discussions about the family/household as a site of world history for more than a decade, and we have worked together on a series of publications related to our joint teaching.[2]

The courses we have taught with a family/household orientation have drawn interest and attention among world historians in the United States, Europe, and China; most recently, we presented a pedagogy workshop at the 2011 meeting of the World History Association in Beijing, along with two University of Minnesota graduate-student TAs and an international undergraduate student.[3]

Our latest venture is a comparative research project that grew directly out of our teaching. The project will examine several dimensions of young women's transition to adulthood in Europe and China: their roles in production and consumption, as well as in systems of marriage and its alternatives. This year we will spend two months in residency at the International Research Center for "Work and Human Lifecycle in Global History" at Humboldt University in Berlin. We plan to focus our research on young women's household and non-household labor (especially as producers of cotton and silk thread and cloth) as they move (or in some cases, don't move) through the life-cycle transition from daughters to wives and from a natal to a marital household. The project will build on existing economic- and demographic-historical work, but our own focus will be the underexplored dimensions of parallels and divergences, namely: family, gender, and generational relations. More to the point, the very conceptualization of this comparative research came to us as we worked together as teachers.

Not all undergraduate classes have the same potential for productive flows between teaching and research. Many course formats, while valuable for imparting knowledge, are not designed to problematize the *production* of knowledge. We would argue for the importance of defending and maintaining a range of pedagogic formats and approaches to teaching so that every professor can engage in teaching that doesn't feel disconnected from his or her "own work." This involves a commitment of resources as well as creative thinking about pedagogy. Large classes must be on the agenda, but classes need to be right-sized and appropriately staffed. Different types of institutions offer different potential in this regard; our colleagues teaching smaller classes in liberal arts colleges, even in some community colleges where section sizes are small, might have an advantage here. But there is also an argument to be made for maximizing the benefits to undergraduates of attending large research universities such as ours by keeping options for research-based teaching open throughout every level of the curriculum. In our experience, such opportunities offer the best option for making our teaching a more integral part of "our own work."

Notes

1. The film clip is available at http://www.youtube.com/watch?v=WH5NZo8Mm0M. For further discussion of this clip, see Barbara Creed and Jeanette Hoorn, "Memory and History: Early Film, Colonialism and the French Civilising Mission in Indochina," in *French History and Civilization. Papers from the George Rudé Seminar*, vol. 4 (2011), edited by Briony Neilson and Robert Aldrich at http://www.h-france.net/rude/rudeTOC2010.html. Creed and Hoorn actually make an argument along the lines we suggest here, similar to the comparison our student drew through the juxtaposition of the clip and the scene from *Martin Guerre*.

2. See, for example, "Women's Life-Cycle Transitions in World-Historical Perspective: Comparing China and Europe," *Journal of Women's History* 12, no. 4 (Winter 2001): 11–21; "Family History as World History" (pamphlet published as part of the American Historical Association series, Women's and Gender History in Global Perspective, 2006); *Family: A World History* (New York: Oxford University Press, 2012); and "Temporalities and Periodization in Deep History: Technology, Gender, and Benchmarks of 'Human Development'" *Social Science History* 36, no. 1 (Spring 2012): 59–83.

3. Emily Bruce, Chen Yueqin, Qin Fang, Ann Waltner, and Mary Jo Maynes, "ROUNDTABLE: Teaching World History as Family History; China as a Case in Point," annual meeting of the World History Association, Beijing, China, July 2011.

The List: What Students Should Know about Federally Funded Historical Research

Bianca Premo

The kind of history I do doesn't normally make news, especially in the United States. But there I was, mentioned in the first line on the front page of the Sunday *Miami Herald*: "A professor at Florida International University won $60,000 to research a rise in litigious Peruvians during the 18th century."[1] When I first saw the article, I lingered over that sentence, putting myself in the place of local readers leaning over the morning paper with their cups of coffee. Were they conjuring an image of professorial me, bespectacled and perhaps hair-bunned, surprised at my front door by a giant check? If they read on, they would find that innocuous image developing into something more sinister.

The article enumerated how the money associated with the 2009 American Recovery and Reinvestment Act, or the "stimulus," was then being spent in Florida. My historical research on everyday litigation and the Enlightenment in the Spanish empire, which had in 2009 received a three-year grant from the National Science Foundation's (NSF) Law and Social Sciences Program, was only one of the article's many examples of stimulus money put to questionable use.[2] Still, the reporter led his piece with my project. He left out of his lead something that I had repeated to him over and over during a phone interview the week before: that my project also involves Spain and Mexico. Mentioning only Peru surely lent greater exoticism to his description of my research. And the idea that federal dollars would be spent on obscure historical themes served the article's subtext: hard-earned tax dollars benefitting opportunists and grifters, including a professor near you.

The reporter undoubtedly discovered my project in a publication that, while less widely read than Miami's main paper, was at least more forthright in its agenda. Shortly before the *Herald* article appeared, my NSF-funded project had found its way to number 51 on a list compiled by Senators John McCain (R-AZ) and Thomas Coburn (R-OK) of the top 100 wasteful uses of stimulus dollars.[3] When ranking my research, they dumped its more traditional academic title and called the project "Law and Order: Spanish Empire." I can only suppose the rechristening was an effort to evoke the sensationalism of a long-running TV drama known for ripping its plots from the headlines. But other than switching the title, the description of my project was ripped straight from my NSF abstract—it being apparently self-evident that research on Spanish imperial history is a waste of money.

This wasn't Sen. Coburn's only attack on NSF social science funding. Around the same time that he and Sen. McCain published their reports against the stimulus, he proposed an amendment to eliminate altogether the agency's funding for political science research, claiming in his speech on the Senate floor that voters could get all the information on politics they wanted from Fox News and CNN, and that political science research would never be funded in the "real world."[4] His statement might well outrage anyone dedicated to the rigors of a discipline and the life of the mind. But when my little project about Spanish imperial law wandered unwittingly onto the front lines of national political debate, I began to think harder about Sen. Coburn's suggestion. More specifically, I realized that his amendment drew from complex national cultural currents, not just partisan struggles over "stimulus" money and the role of government but also from some fundamental American beliefs and practices (some might say "discourses") about education and educators, research and the "real world."

Americans seem inveterately distrustful of intellectual authority and unusually enamored of auto-didacticism. Maybe it is the country's dominant Protestantism, which shunned the authority of priests as the sole interpreters of sacred texts. Maybe it's the Enlightenment roots of our nation, which shunned the authority of sacred texts. In any case, it was an American thinker, Ralph Waldo Emerson, who suggested that after being "shut up in schools and college recitation rooms," we emerge with a "bellyful of words ... not know[ing] a thing." For Emerson, every man was a scholar whose education in nature and action was "better than books." The persistence of this strain of thought struck me as I perused some responses to a news-website piece about the "top 10 most unemployable majors." Many readers expressed outrage at the "uselessness" of undergraduate degrees and echoed the great Transcendentalist's belief that students who felt they'd learned something life-altering in a college classroom could have gained the same experience reading "the same books" on their own.

Indeed, Americans have a special fondness for innovators and entrepreneurs who, like Steve Jobs, were misfits in school but succeeded in the "real world." That romance crosses the aisle: only a few months after Coburn and McCain began issuing their stimulus Lists, the Obama administration attached a public relations initiative to its 2011 budget proposal entitled "Winning the Future."[5] But the initiative did not treat innovation and institutional education (or institutional funding) as adversaries. Rather, it married public investment in educational institutions, scholarly innovation, and infrastructural investment, and doubled research and development dollars to granting agencies like the NSF.

The "Winning the Future" meme departed from the news cycle as quickly as it entered (hastened, no doubt, by its unfortunate acronym). But it left vexing questions. Even a presidential administration that supports federal funding for research subsumes the endeavor within the national(ist) context of job creation, applied science, and technology. Had I let my country down by taking money that really should go to the inventor of the next Internet? Had I contributed to the misery of America's unemployed by robbing someone of a job in wind-based energy? Was my research on colonial Spanish America really relevant enough to compete for federal dollars?

Reflecting on these questions, I came to the conclusion that scholars with public funding had not been maligned so much as misunderstood. What The List concealed, first and foremost, is that I had not applied for "stimulus" money *per se*. In fact, when I applied to the small program within the National Science Foundation that annually funds research on the law and social sciences, there was no such thing as a "stimulus." It was pure happenstance that the following year, as my application successfully made its way through the review process, so-called stimulus money replenished the NSF's coffers to pre-9/11 levels.[6] I realized that nonacademics may not know that professors rely heavily (if indirectly) on tax dollars for research in ordinary times, and that the stimulus did not create a windfall for "new" projects, but simply kept the system afloat. I suppose that the NSF could have called for "stimulus"-style proposals and evaluated them with entirely new, jobs-oriented criteria (and, indeed, the positions for graduate research assistants I hired were reported as "jobs created"). But this would have significantly shifted the agency's long-standing, rigorous definitions of scientific merit. And it is difficult to see how the year-long anonymous review process that proposals undergo to assess scholarly merit could be reconciled with an economic program whose goal was to pump money into the economy quickly.

I will return to the implications of the peer review process momentarily, but first a word on how political definitions of "merit" are derived from the commonsense notion that research should result in some immediate and tangible product, stamped with "Made in the USA" and recognizably valuable to any taxpayer. Such notions sidestep the reality that knowledge production is not only incremental but also transnational. Beyond the specifics of my project as "stimulus" lay insinuations about the obscurity of my research, as history and especially as non-US history. Obviously, most dollars in federally funded programs do not flow to historians of Latin America. In fact, it is rare to find any historians ever funded by the NSF. Within the Law and Social Science Program, funding typically goes to law school faculty and doctoral students who research the US. In 2009, even research on US law consumed few stimulus funds: the entire Law and Social Sciences Program received, by my calculations, only .0017 percent of the Recovery Act funding provided to the NSF (which was, in turn, only one-third of its budget), and the program overall received a mere .000006 percent of all Recovery Act funds.[7] I was thus particularly proud to get an NSF grant since it meant that I had successfully translated my project outside of my regional and disciplinary fields to argue for its wider significance to the social sciences.

What is more, on the face of things the wider significance of my project should have appealed to conservatives like Coburn and McCain. My book will demonstrate how free and enslaved, male and female, rich and poor Spanish American legal subjects were invested in Enlightenment notions of equality, popular sovereignty, and even nascent free markets. Such arguments should not raise the hackles of those politicians who relentlessly promote unreconstructed ideas from 19th-century classical liberalism. Maybe it wasn't the historical but rather the "foreign" nature of the project that was so self-evidently objectionable. To be sure, a similar project on Enlightenment legal practices among colonists and slaves in the Thirteen Colonies—let's call it "Law and Order: The Great American Version"—might still have made The List. But I cannot help thinking that, to the list makers, the non-national nature of my study enhanced its irrelevance. (The students at my own public university, over 65 percent of whom are Latino, might not be so readily convinced of its irrelevance or "non-national" character, regardless of their own political commitments. Many of our history majors are interested in entering our new law school to study both US common- and Latin American civil-law traditions.)

Perhaps arguing about the relative value of research—national, historical, or otherwise—with this crowd is futile. Maybe it is not so much the research that needs explaining as the processes through which it is judged, funded, and published. The List forced me to confront the fact that I had indeed been wasting something. Not money, but the opportunity to explain what I do—what *we* do as historians—to the American "public" I encounter every day: students.

In addition to teaching students what we know, I realize now that we must teach them what we do and how we do it. That is to say, undergraduates must be told, over and over, that the history books they read, the lectures they hear, and the documents they find in the library and on the Internet do not appear *sui generis*. It is not obvious to them that historical research is overwhelmingly a product of *the labor* of *individuals*—not of the "government," and not of abstract institutions—even when federally funded. And it is not at all obvious to them that most good history is the product of processes and qualities that even the sharpest critic of "big government" reveres: innovation, merit, entrepreneurial spirit, investment, and, most importantly within the American cultural lexicon, competition.

Students should know that promotion and tenure at most universities and colleges rest heavily on individual initiative in research. They might not like it. They might think that our research has little to do with them. They might believe that brilliant researchers are too distracted to care about teaching. But whether or not we want to defend the importance of research at most colleges and universities (and many of the examples of the synergy between teaching and research that appear in this volume will provide evidence that we need to do just that), for now, that is the way it is. Even faculty who work in institutions where merit in teaching is paramount or who are not required to publish (such as underpaid adjuncts) must rely on publishing historian-educators for the materials they use in courses. Modern-day Emersons wishing to bypass teachers and institutions altogether, and just read "history" on their own, cannot do so without someone willing to conduct research and publish it.

Students at public institutions in particular need to know that universities do not dole out unlimited (or oftentimes *any*) funds for faculty to research and disseminate their work—even though faculty productivity and excellence in research is the primary criteria used to rate their "value" to the institution. This is especially true for faculty in heavy "service teaching" departments in the humanities and social sciences, who are the least likely to have stable university-provided research funds. In addition, students—including and perhaps especially graduate students—need to know that most faculty are paid on a nine-month schedule, in part to ensure that scholars have time to engage in the research and writing on which their performance is judged. Students armed with such knowledge might then recognize how the drive to seek research funds beyond our institutions, and oftentimes beyond our discipline, is built into the very structure of academic employment.

Finally, students should understand that highly competitive federal (and private) fellowships and grants for research make up the difference. This is especially true for pioneering historical research that draws on documents not available in published or electronic form. Put differently, scholars who still do fieldwork, and who must travel to undertake archival research, rely heavily on federal funds. Students must understand that such historians engage in agonizing, seemingly endless rounds of competition to secure funding and to publish their research. Even during the comparatively flush year I received my NSF grant, the agency rejected the proposals of around 70 percent of all applicants. In the processes of selection, the agency counted on the labor of over 46,000 expert external reviewers, who spent hours poring over the applications and selecting meritorious projects by applying criteria that included the proposals' scientific rigor and their utility to all Americans. These experts—and others like them reviewing grant proposals for federal and private agencies, scholarly journals and presses, and for the universities who must seek outside evaluations to tenure and promote their faculty— perform this labor *for free*. Thus, the employment of experts in ensuring the merit of funded research, published scholarship, and academic advancement is an area of our profession that does not conform to one of the most sacred of American values: the market ethos. And it doesn't cost taxpayers a dime.

In the end, getting NSF funding for my research affected my teaching in the obvious ways: by enabling me to perform historical research and to share, in turn, the documents, methods, and lessons of history with my students. Turning up on The List for that NSF funding affected my teaching in less obvious ways, making me rethink how I educate American students—not so much about history as about what historians, and all professors, do in the "real world" of competitive research funding.

Notes

1. Douglas Hanks, "Where Florida's Stimulus Money Has Gone, From $200 Million for Electric Meters to $302.50 for New Threads, How the Stimulus Money Was—And Still Is—Being Allocated in Florida," *Miami Herald*, September 26, 2010.

2. My project received $59,845 over three years, around 29 percent of which went directly to my university for state-mandated cost sharing. The remainder paid for my travel to archives, two months of summer salary, and the employment of graduate research assistants in the US who cataloged the first comparative data ever collected on litigation in the empire.

3. Sen. Tom Coburn, MD, and Senator John McCain, Senate Report, "Summertime Blues: 100 Stimulus Projects That Give Taxpayers the Blues," August 2010, http://coburn.senate.gov/public//index.cfm?a=Files.Serve&File_id=a7e82141-1a9e-4eec-b160-6a8e62427efb. Note that, in a circular reference, Sen. Coburn's website in turn linked to the *Herald* report, which undoubtedly drew in part from the senator's own original list, http://coburn.senate.gov/public/index.cfm/2010/9/where-florida-s-stimulus-money-has-gone.

4. Joseph Uscinski and Casey A. Klofstad, "Who Likes Political Science? Determinants of Senators' Votes on the Coburn Amendment," *PS: Political Science and Politics* (2010): 701–706. The October 13, 2009, Senate session in which HR 2847 was discussed can be viewed at http://www.c-spanarchives.org/program/289431-1. Also see the *Chronicle of Higher Education*'s coverage, http://chronicle.com/article/Senator-Proposes-an-End-to/48746.

5. The budget proposal and rationale are found at http://www.whitehouse.gov/winning-the-future.

6. Total NSF funding in 2009 was $9.5 billion, 3 billion of which was provided by the American Recovery and Reinvestment Act. It is worth noting that this was not an unprecedented budget for the agency; the infusion of "stimulus" money simply returned NSF spending to the same levels it had enjoyed in 2000. Figures come from the document, "United States National Science Foundation FY 2009 Performance and Financial Highlights," http://www.nsf.gov/publications/pub_summ.jsp?ods_key=nsf10002.

7. The program received around $4.77 million of the 3 billion provided to the agency as part of the Recovery Act (whose total I consider to be 789 billion). I made this calculation using the "FY 2009 Performance and Financial Highlights," and the NSF Law and Social Sciences interactive map of funding accessible from http://www.nsf.gov/funding/pgm_summ.jsp?pims_id=5422.

Teaching in the Archive: What the Professor Learned

Kathi Kern

We have all done it. We have all had our "Ferris Bueller" moment. Or perhaps I am merely coming clean here, confessing my sins, guilty of the impure pleasures of lecturing. Temporarily mesmerized by the power of my own performance, I have caught myself, usually not quite in time. "Ask a question," the inner voice of my active-learning higher self urges. And so I do. And then, as though on cue, I hear myself utter those fateful lines from the 1986 film *Ferris Bueller's Day Off*: "Anyone? Anyone?!"

The problem is, I know better. Granted, we lecture for good, sometimes even noble reasons: because we want to convey our passion for history and frame our students' learning by synthesizing massive amounts of information. Frankly (if less nobly), we also lecture because we confront escalating class sizes. But as Mary Jo Maynes and Ann Waltner argue in this volume, the lecture does not have to be a passive learning experience for students. We can use lectures as an opportunity to simulate historical thinking processes. But do we?

Tom Holt's *Thinking Historically: Narrative, Imagination, and Understanding* provided me with useful advice as a young teacher. After interviewing high school students who seemed disengaged from History as a discipline, Professor Holt sought to interrogate their alienation. I was particularly drawn to his description of Debbie, a senior at a vocational high school who nailed the problem: history (she said) was "someone else's facts." For Debbie, as for the other students Holt interviewed, the dominion of "facts" in the teaching of history closed off the possibility of investment, creativity, and imagination. At best, students writing history could arrange (or rearrange) "someone else's facts." Based on his interviews and his own teaching experience, Holt became convinced that "even younger and less prepared students can be engaged in a more active and imaginative examination of what history offers."[1]

After 20 years of teaching history at a large state university, I still watch with frustration as students struggle to make the transition from upper-level content-driven courses to seminars in which they are expected to conduct their own research. I've come to believe that the struggle is ours, as faculty, to better unveil the practice of historical research in our lower level classes. When Tom Holt published *Thinking Historically* in 1990, the idea of shelving the textbook and teaching history armed only with primary sources bordered on revolutionary. We have long since changed our tune, and teaching with primary sources is now a routine strategy in both higher education and the precollegiate classroom. As disciplinary practitioners, we continue to experiment with the most effective way of integrating primary sources. In recent years, a number of significant collaborative research projects have emerged to explore that practice and to illuminate the metacognitive skills historians hope to enhance in their students.[2]

At the same time, our students' increased exposure to primary sources has not always deepened their understanding of the ways historians find, understand, and make use of those sources. Bolstered by the availability of primary-source readers, web sites, and other auxiliary materials provided by textbook companies, teachers of history typically select a source or two, ask students to locate the sources in time and place, and lead them in a "close reading" of the documents. Keith Barton argues that such an exercise should not be misconstrued as simulating authentic historical practice. Historians, Barton contends, do not use sources in the ways modeled in "document-based activities." For that matter, historians would rarely invoke the phrase "primary sources," except in a bibliography. Rather, historians talk in terms of "questions" and "evidence."[3] Too much of the authentic practice of historians gets obscured in "document-based activities." Professional historians rarely base an argument on only a handful of documents. Furthermore, one of the essential practices of a historian—evaluating the use of evidence by other historians—is too rarely replicated in history classrooms. Barton underscores the limitations of isolating individual sources out of context.

My intervention described here has its own limitations, but I want to make a pitch for inviting college students, at all levels, into the archive. My remaining comments focus on how my students reacted to an assignment that required them to spend one class period in the archives. The project did not simulate historical research in every way: the assignment was carefully scaffolded to be completed in one class; students worked in teams focused on a single collection; the archivist culled the collections to identify the most pertinent materials; and the students were required to emerge from the archive with a solid historical question, not an argument or a thesis. Still, I would venture my students learned more about historical practice in that one class than in everything else we did in the balance of the semester.

In one of the archival projects from which my examples will be drawn, students looked at a very small collection of sources connected to the life of Belle Brezing (1860–1940), a legendary brothel owner in Lexington, Kentucky. Widely believed to be the inspiration for the fictional character of Belle Watling in Margaret Mitchell's *Gone with the Wind*, Brezing left behind little in the way of traditional archival fare. Students pieced together aspects of Brezing's life and business based largely on ephemera: photographs, one scrapbook, interviews with two of Belle's "working girls," and media coverage—including an obituary in *Time* magazine. An extraordinary aspect of the collection is several pieces of Brezing's wardrobe. The archivist supplemented this thin collection with the kinds of sources historians might consult: census data, Sanborn insurance maps, and city directories. Given the limited time to complete the assignment, we posed questions for the students to answer, moving from simple observations ("Use the Sanborn maps to determine the size and structure of Brezing's property") to more complex questions ("What can you determine about the class and racial composition of the surrounding neighborhood?"). With the absence of either a "master narrative" or the rich textual sources historians often use to build a narrative (diaries, letters, etc.), students were freed to pose their own questions about a rich life's fragmented remains.

Having now taken students to the archives for several years, I am convinced that Tom Holt is correct: students are capable of more active and imaginative engagement in historical practice. I base my conclusions on the anonymous written assessments that students produced after their archival visit, as well as from an in-depth interview I conducted with a focus group composed of former students who volunteered to help with this piece.

Students reported a sense of excitement and discovery. Despite his critique of some document-based activities, Barton stresses that one of the best reasons to expose students to primary sources is to "motivate historical inquiry."[4] My students concur. Part of the excitement lay simply in discovering the easy availability of the archives. Prior to the mandatory assignment in my class, many students were unaware of the collections, or "did not know who was allowed to look at the archives." Even after I convinced them that they were certainly "allowed" in the archives, students reported an "intimidating atmosphere." The rules that professional historians take for granted—signing in, showing identification, placing personal items in a locker, using a pencil—can feel unwelcoming to a generation of digital natives who cut their teeth on "open access." As one student explained: "If I weren't meeting you here, I probably would have walked back out. Once that lady questioned me, I would have been like: 'you know what, I'm good,' and left."

Once launched on their archival projects, students found that the work itself inspired their curiosity. Kelsey, a middle-school education major, explained: "I had never experienced anything like this before, so it took me a while, when I first saw all the documents I was a little overwhelmed, so once I got into it and I ... figured out how to pace myself and what to look for, that really helped." Sarah, a law school-bound senior in political science was not an easy convert to archival work: "Honestly, at first, I hated the idea of it. I thought it was going to be super boring and not worth my time, but then, once you start looking at the photographs, I mean, I had never done it before. It just opened up a whole new world of history and a different way of looking at things, and having a more critical analysis of things." Sarah concluded that the Belle Brezing archive "brought history to life."

Students engaged in inquiry and problem solving, and gained practice at forming historical questions. Even with the fragmentary evidence of the Belle Brezing Collection, students posed significant historical questions. They focused first of all on the property Belle owned at 59 Megowan Street. Using the Sanborn Insurance maps, students pointed out that Brezing's house stood on one of the largest lots in the neighborhood. The house itself was brick, whereas the surrounding houses were frame and listed on the maps as female boarding houses. In the midst of this "low-end" neighborhood, students pointed out, sat Belle's elegant property. Photographs of the home's interior revealed a Victorian style of decorating, complete with expensive drapery, art, and pottery—the visual culture of middle-class respectability. That theme of "respectability" was echoed, my students suggested, by Belle's "high-end" wardrobe and her insistence on "decorum" in her business practices. As Sarah said: "It just makes me wonder what her motives were for wanting to remain in that area. I mean, she was in a profession that did not offer a lot of dignity, [yet] she has nice clothes, nice house, was interested in art and she's obviously a successful businesswoman ... . [This] just makes me want to look further into it, into why she was involved in prostitution in the first place." Lane, a history major, reinforced the idea of respectability in Brezing's business practice. "Those interviews we looked at," Lane observed, made clear that "all parties involved, the ladies and the gentlemen in the parlors had to be polite and civilized." In one case, working girls were sitting outside cross-legged, "and their skirts were at their knees and Belle said: 'they should be arrested for that.'" "She wanted the outer world to think she was elegant and civilized," Lane concluded. Phil, a future social studies teacher, agreed: "Belle definitely had the money to move, if she wanted to. Even when her house burned down, she decided to rebuild there and not to move to a 'better' part of town when it was pretty obvious she had the money. I think part of it is that even though she was a high-end prostitute, people still understood that she was a prostitute, and so I think she kind of felt obligated [to stay]. ... And the fact that she was probably bringing in higher-end clients, you don't want your high-end clients walking around their high-end neighborhoods walking to a known prostitute's house."

Students practiced linking historical thinking concepts to the raw material of the archives. The students' discussion of prostitution and "respectability" was organic and unprompted. Their spontaneous conversation reminded me that students bring all kinds of prior knowledge into our classrooms. Typically, they expose their own investments in the process of analyzing the past. Occasionally, they reveal powerfully embedded myths that we, as their teachers, attempt to disrupt. In this assignment, I was encouraged by the students' discussion of "respectability" and the ways that the archival collection expanded their understanding of the concept. At my prompting, students also discussed the concept of "agency," arguing that even with the partial nature of the collection's evidence, Brezing's agency could be detected. Phil pointed out that when Brezing was interviewed by the census taker, she did not reply to most of the questions posed, refusing to answer queries about birth, occupation, and national origin. "She didn't answer anything until it came to the part where, well, can you read and write? And then she put 'yes' but she didn't answer any of the other questions. It's kind of like she wanted to make a point that she was educated."

Students gained a better understanding of the practice of research. On evaluations of the archival project, students assessed the value of the exercise in uncovering the process of research. One student explained: "So often in history classes we only look at the results of historians' research but this project allowed me to see firsthand where research begins and it was very beneficial." Students grew more sympathetic to the work of historians. According to another student: "The value to a student is actually getting a hands-on approach to history and getting a real insight into what kind of challenges face a historian when trying to collect information." As Phil put it (and others agreed), looking at the archival collection was much more engaging than reading the seemingly "finished" work of a history textbook: "You would never get this information from reading a textbook ... until you actually see it going through [Belle's] scrapbook, looking through her pictures, you don't really understand that though she was a prostitute, she definitely had agency. She definitely had wealth. She was definitely educated."

Students also gained a better understanding of the archive's limitations. In the case of the Belle Brezing Collection, students accessed an archive largely untouched by historians. For my students, the archive inspired more questions than it answered. One particularly intriguing piece of evidence is Brezing's scrapbook, given to her as a teenager by the man who first seduced her. Sarah wrote:

> I found the scrapbook really fascinating ... . There were several poems throughout there, but one was actually signed, I mean, her name underneath, so I'm assuming she wrote it. And there were several other poems throughout, so that could have been a way of expressing herself. And she got one published in a newspaper. And in the back, it was almost like a yearbook, because some of her schoolmates had signed and written little endearments about her. It makes me think that maybe her scrapbook was a way, a form of expression, that maybe she carried it around with her. That's where she kept a bunch of mementos. You can see the glue marks and the fingerprints, and so, it just suggested a lot of things. When you think of a prostitute, you don't think that they're interested in art, in nature, and she seemed to find beauty in just about everything she did and I think that's reflected in her poetry and her scrapbook.

Students emerged from the assignment with a sense of ownership of the research process. Students resoundingly applauded the invitation to enter into a conversation among historians. One student's anonymous comment was echoed by virtually all the students in my focus group: "I felt like I was teaching myself and was able to make my own assumptions, which was refreshing." Zachary, who is preparing to be a high school teacher, located the value of the archival exercise in its success at moving students out of the position of passive learners: "we are given the opportunity to find what we believe to be significant." Sarah too found this aspect rewarding because it "lets you create your own personal interpretation of the history instead of reading just facts or someone else's view on the history. It also lets you move at your own pace and research more into topics that are particularly interesting to you and you may not get from reading a book or listening to a lecture." Lane too liked being part of the process: "I feel like you're helping discover and search for history, rather than just reading about what somebody has found in history."

My students' reactions demonstrate the value of archival research to undergraduate training in history. Archival work should not be hoarded, reserved only for majors completing capstone courses en route to graduation. Rather, the lessons drawn from this one archival exercise should inspire us to build archival research opportunities into every level of the curriculum.

Acknowledgments

The archival projects for my history classes were suggested and conceptualized by Kate Black, the curator of the Appalachian Collection at the University of Kentucky Special Collections and Archives. Without her facility with the collections and creative teaching strategies, this exercise would not have been the profound experience it was for my students. I am also grateful to the University of Kentucky Libraries for their willingness to see students as researchers and to allow entirely too many of us to descend upon the archives at one time. My thanks to the five students who participated in the focus group: Zachary Chesser, Kelsey Farr, Phillip Hyde, Sarah Houseman, and Lane Springer. Finally, I offer thanks to my research assistant, David Andrew Lai, for transcribing the interviews, and to Antoinette Burton and Kate Black for feedback and encouragement.

Notes

1. Tom Holt, *Thinking Historically: Narrative, Imagination, and Understanding* (New York: College Board, 1990), 18.

2. See, for example, the Stanford University project Reading like a Historian, http://sheg.stanford.edu/?q=node/45, and the Indiana University History Learning Project, http://www.iub.edu/~hlp.

3. Keith Barton, "Primary Sources in History: Breaking Through the Myths," *Phi Delta Kappan* 86, no. 10 (June 2005): 745–53.

4. Barton, "Primary Sources in History," 751.

"Spare the Messenger": Envisioning a Future for Teacher-Historians

John Ramsbottom

Several months ago, an extraordinary e-mail appeared in my inbox. The writer was a former undergraduate history student at an American university who had subsequently returned to China. Somewhere among my tracks left on the Internet, he had detected my interest in teaching the course US History as World History. He invited my attention to the website he had created for a proposed course to be taught online and based entirely on comparisons between feature films and the historical eras they portray, from *Ben Hur* to *Saving Private Ryan*. Lack of both time and technological competence—not to mention wariness about the ramifications of copyright law—prevented me from responding with more than simple courtesy. But in the context of a discussion about the future of history teaching, this trivial incident underscores a noteworthy point: in the coming decades, the adage "everyone his or her own historian" will apply not just to the transformative power of history but also to its global reach.

As a group, historians may be forgiven for believing that the values of academic freedom, critical reflection, and multicultural awareness should flourish in an era of unprecedented international communication. That the practice of history might cease to be primarily a literary pastime of a privileged, largely Western elite, and become instead a fundamental attitude of mind around the globe, is an exhilarating thought. But from the perspective of a long-time teacher like myself, one whose career has taken him to a half-dozen liberal arts colleges and universities, the waning influence of academic history is troubling. Study after study in the AHA's *Perspectives on History* shows that increasing competition for fewer jobs has inflicted damage on the profession's morale. We must also contemplate the damage done to its effectiveness. Equipping rising generations with the tools and insights afforded by historical study will require that we refine and target our message. But we must also accept the obligation to nurture and sustain our messengers. The prevailing standards of professional advancement make these tasks more difficult.

The greatest threat to the future health of the discipline arises from the gradual looming collapse of humanities education generally; among the liberal arts, history faces a particularly stiff challenge to justify its place in the college curriculum. On the one hand, the study of history may seem pleasing but hardly essential: everyone keeps handy some invariable "lesson of history," even if the details of the events that demonstrate it remain fuzzy. On the other hand, the contributions of academic history may appear insufficiently practical or downright harmful. English departments can assert their utility by offering courses in composition and rhetoric; in a national emergency, knowledge of certain foreign languages becomes "critical"— witness the demand for speakers of Arabic or Pashtun—and so forth. Because the methods and conclusions of history appear commonsensical and familiar, the public can feel a sense of ownership. But when historians produce innovative research that questions popular truths, the discipline can then be portrayed as outside the mainstream, undeserving of support.

As if to counteract the impression that members of the history faculty are either tiresome *raconteurs* or ivory-tower radicals, institutions in every corner of higher education increasingly tout an image of the scholar-teacher. By remaining actively engaged in the production of higher scholarship, they suggest, the historian is able to bring students the benefits of up-to-date knowledge in the field, while personally exemplifying intellectual rigor and creativity. Thus, the pursuit of research is regarded as much more than an earned reward or a valid outlet for curiosity; it is indispensable to good teaching. But this notion is subject to a couple of qualifications. The first is that, with few exceptions, the putative interaction between archive and classroom is seldom direct. Society needs accomplished historical researchers—they are scholars and artists of a high order—but they do not all have to pursue their craft in an academic setting, nor are undergraduates their principal audience. Moreover, it's rarely the case that one's current research matters to the content of a survey course, though it might influence someone else's teaching ten years hence. Second is a fact even more subversive of the scholar-teacher ideal: the historians most frequently in contact with college students are also those least able to engage in research and writing.

Part-time and adjunct faculty, assisted by graduate students, now carry the major portion of the "teaching load" (the terminology is suggestive) at the largest institutions serving the largest cohorts of undergraduates. While fulfilling a vital function within the school's overall mission, and often one of particular importance to the humanities, these instructors are also under pressure to produce traditional scholarship. Except for graduate students, the object of this exercise is not to demonstrate intellectual ability—many of these faculty have long since published a monograph and more—nor is it to give evidence of continued growth as a scholar, since, to put it bluntly, no one is evaluating them for the purpose of granting tenure. Instead, faculty on temporary contracts can find themselves compelled to publish chiefly for the sake of attracting alternative job offers—since that is the recognized currency of the academic marketplace—risking burnout in an effort to demonstrate their value. Is this a proper or rational approach to building a corps of dedicated historian-teachers, able and willing to respond to the opportunities presented by globalizing history?

In a period of abundant labor, shrinking budgets, and stable enrollments, no incentive compels history departments to consider revising the existing standards of professional excellence; on the contrary, there is inadequate room for those already qualified. By endorsing the traditional model of tenure, academic administrators perpetuate the reliance on "contingent" faculty to do much of the actual teaching, in conditions of insecure employment, scant job benefits, and limited support for research. This is the reality confronted by most non-tenured faculty, whose ranks I willingly joined in 2001. In my own prior experience—by no means typical at the time and virtually inconceivable now—it had proved possible to gain tenure without producing a steady stream of publications. Equally important, even after I had tenure, on-going research was encouraged, both rhetorically and financially. Scholarship mattered mostly because it served to stimulate my thinking about the practice of history, whether it resulted in a conference paper or a new upper-level seminar. When, for family reasons, I sought to change institutions, I was concerned primarily about whether an adjunct position would provide comparable intellectual challenges.

A dozen years on, I can say that it has. In the relatively enlightened history department where I first fetched up as an adjunct, the only restriction on my full participation was time itself. I discovered an academic history community extending beyond higher education to other arenas of rapid change, for example, the AP curriculum and secondary-teacher development. Instead of remaining oppressed by the expectation that they will be treated as second-tier colleagues, nontenured historians should be empowered to contribute fully to their current institutions. In terms that should make sense to a manager in Human Resources, the failure to make full use of their accumulated experience has been a waste. Particularly in the midst of the current crisis, they represent valuable assets.

Historians share with other humanists an outlook essential to the survival of the liberal arts generally. As one undergraduate student of mine elegantly expressed it, "There are many ways to study human beings. History is the one I find most congenial." This is the sort of response that our teaching must inspire, whether in four-year institutions, community colleges, libraries, or high schools. There is an urgent need for a timely, effective, and affordable investment in the skills of teacher-historians. Career-paths that lead to positions as adjunct or part-time faculty should not be perceived as the unfortunate outcome of "oversupply" but rather as deliberately constructed alternatives to the conventional tenure-track.

Twenty years ago, a colleague told me that the most important issue facing higher education was "access." At the time, this seemed overly dramatic—after all, the "echo" of the boomers would not strike for another decade. In fact, he was not referring to the impending strain on physical plants or funding, much less the contemporary scandal of unsustainable borrowing for college. He was talking simply about student access to faculty and, through them, to the life of the mind. Today, when one of our students' principal concerns is "getting" enough courses to finish a degree in four years, and efforts to establish a course sequence within the major are hampered by a shortage of "seats" in lower-level prerequisites, his remark seems positively prescient. Right now, history needs every messenger we can muster, and an ample reservoir of able practitioners waits to be called upon.

In my own view, what undergraduates need most from their teachers is a model of complex and complete thinking. Historians know that thorough understanding follows tracing-out a mental map of research—an insight that historians at all levels can bring to the classroom. Some of the most effective pedagogy may well take place when instructors are freed from the demands of publication in order to focus on what works in the classroom. When the task of teaching is entrusted largely to graduate students, they not only develop their skills in discussion sections, but also learn to love the process. As the essay by Maynes and Waltner in this volume suggests, however, even large-scale lectures can take the form of posing a question, identifying possible evidence, and sifting it for conclusions. In both settings, students can consider the importance of context, authorship, and audience.

If this approach sounds old-fashioned—and no doubt it is—the steadily lengthening list of titles in the Bedford/St. Martin's series Brief History with Documents testifies to its vitality.

A fruitful future for history will also mean taking seriously the implications of evolving technology for both teaching and research. Any historian who doubts the potential of the marketplace to shape the purpose and content of our discipline should pause to note the prominence of a "history" tab on the web portal of every business, for-profit or not, and the ubiquity of online slogans like "world's leading education company." Keeping in mind the role of new media in widening the influence of history everywhere, the criteria for academic performance should be re-defined. Some graduate departments have already been prodded by the expertise of their own students to recognize a range of digital modes of research and publication. In the same context, it makes sense to supplement standard historiography courses with an introduction to not only hyperlinked subject bibliographies and critically annotated databases but also other tools that are less readily associated with history—Geographic Information Systems, data-mining, and social media—but which are already making an impact on our undergraduates.

The utility of technology can also be leveraged through a judicious use of "distance learning." To some veteran teachers (until recently, myself included), this online system of "course delivery" can seem the antithesis of everything the liberal arts stand for. What place is there for the shared exploration of texts, the discursive conversation, or, for that matter, the personal example of the mentor? Nevertheless, persuaded that it might have some promise, I agreed to condense an existing 15-week survey of pre-modern Britain into eight highly structured lessons. The typical week's work consisted of a slide-illustrated lecture, a short primary source exercise, an interpretive essay based on required reading, and an assignment using Internet resources. In addition, I "met" with students online via video conferencing to debate events such as the trial of Charles I. Students had to submit not only written assignments but also, on one occasion, a recorded audio "newscast" about the Battle of Hastings. In this way, almost all of the reading in the course was connected to a particular short-term "work product," a method congenial to students' understanding of how "the real world" operates. When I met the class face-to-face at the end of the course and graded the final exam, I found many of my impressions confirmed. Many evinced a clear preference for the online setting—not only those who made use of the technology to participate in relative anonymity, but also those who remained engaged across the board.

If online teaching worked for a baby-boomer like me, younger historians will gain even more—particularly given their greater facility with the necessary technology. More to the point, one can envision a group of adjunct or part-time faculty working together online to develop a "distance-learning" course, initially perhaps for their own campus, to which each contributes a brief video-lecture or primary source assignment based on his or her own interests and research. Such an arrangement would exploit the special knowledge of several participants while allowing them to collaborate remotely; regular meetings at a coffee shop would be optional. As for the vexed question of who owns the resulting course material: that will arise inevitably as the digital revolution proceeds, whether or not history reaps the advantages. We cannot allow it to pose an insuperable obstacle.

In history, things change slowly. Too many graduate students and young PhDs still aspire to an ideal of the academic life inherited from the era when full professors were middle-aged men whose spouses formed the corps of "faculty wives" or, more distantly, when scholars were mostly solitary males if not actually monks. Combined with severe financial constraints, the traditional quest for tenure excludes many trained historians from stable employment and undermines our ability to face the manifold challenges confronting our profession. At the same time, global technological change has shifted the horizons of historical inquiry at home and abroad, opening unimagined possibilities for collaboration and understanding. In these circumstances, redefining the image of the scholar-teacher is not abandoning the historian's calling, but reinforcing and enriching it. Simply defending the *status quo* could leave us with a discipline that is rightly viewed as irrelevant.

Race and Feminisms in Slavery's Archive

Jennifer L. Morgan

Students come to my classes for a variety of reasons, but many are trying to locate a kind of grounding for their own histories and a tool for understanding their experience of race and racism. While I urge my students to use the past to think critically about the present, I am also (sometimes painfully) aware of the lure of foreclosure: the notion that the 400-year history of Atlantic slavery can be condensed into an image of a 19th-century Big House, or that the link between slavery and video vixens is obvious. I find myself actively counteracting their impulse to make easy connections between past and present by insisting instead on historical specificity, on the particularities of time and space, on the infinite flexibility of an institution that functioned on vast sugar plantations and small family farms, on board ships and in the middle of growing cities, among hundreds of other enslaved people, and amidst profound and alienating isolation—in other words, by insisting that we act like historians.

A disciplinary certainty attends much of my teaching, but my institutional location has always been more complicated. From my first job at Rutgers University to my position today at New York University, I have always been jointly appointed: at Rutgers in the History Department and the Department of Women's and Gender Studies; at NYU in the Department of Social and Cultural Analysis (which houses, among other things, Africana Studies, American Studies, and Gender Sexuality Studies) and the Department of History. I have always seen these appointments as beneficial, as an institutional location that supported both my scholarship and my teaching. And yet, I approached my teaching from an initial position that can only be characterized as deeply segregated. At Rutgers I actually had the luxury of two offices, one in each department, separated by a mile-long trek from College Avenue to Douglass College. There, I cleaved my book collection in half, imposing an increasingly untenable logic to keep the "gender" books separate from the "race and slavery" books. You'll know where this is going—it was the deluded act of a very young intellect, and one I view with incredulity from the safety of my newly integrated office space here at NYU.

Placing texts together, both on my bookshelf and in the classroom, was a symbolic gesture that spoke to a more complicated process. In women's studies classrooms, my initial goals were simple: to expand students' sense of gender as a singular technology of repression and liberation. This was an exercise that challenged but did not surprise students in women's studies classrooms in the late 1990s. Entering the field at this historical juncture meant that the crucial interventions of the Combahee River Collective and the burgeoning Women of Color feminism exemplified by Kitchen Table Press and *This Bridge Called My Back* were firmly a part of the classroom's lexicon, even if students still struggled with the unmodified category of "Woman" in ways that undergirded the 1983 publication *All the Women Are White, All the Blacks are Men: But Some of Us Are Brave*.[1]

For many years, I have taught a version of a course on black feminisms or the feminist writings of women of color for which Kimberle Crenshaw's concept of intersectionality has formed the organizing principal.[2] Crenshaw's work has been absolutely central in the elaboration of a black feminist theoretic, and as such has been widely influential, if often poorly elaborated. Crenshaw's widely echoed call to understand as simultaneous the problems of race, gender, and class is deceptively simple—in part because students often believe the three categories were once distinct and are only now (post-Crenshaw) in need of integration. In other words, they believe the task at hand is to simply keep the three balls simultaneously in the air, rather than understand that the motion itself defines the problem, and that three (or more) distinct categories never existed.

In my history courses (such as the first half of the African American history survey or Caribbean Slavery), the greatest challenge was to refuse the historical distance students constructed in which to find refuge. Moreover, students quite capable of thinking about slavery as an economic and social institution fumbled when asked to discuss the ways in which that institution was gendered; slavery may have occasionally happened to women but was not an institution built upon a particular ideological or material positionality of women. As I led students through readings and sources in which assumptions about women's reproductive lives were embedded in the racial logic that undergirded the practice of trans-Atlantic slavery, I battled against a commonly held presumption that these courses—logged as they were under American history or African American history—represented a subject matter outside the women's history rubric. That courses on American slavery did not count towards women's history majors or concentrations was a source of considerable frustration, but the impulse that had me separating my bookshelves carried over into the way I thought about my teaching and my scholarship—the frustration felt distinct from my larger work as a researcher and a writer. Even as I corralled the sense that something was out of kilter with how I managed my teaching, I forged ahead on my scholarship.

In retrospect, the tensions I experienced across the curriculum helped me to craft my manuscript: as I muddled through the arguments of what became *Laboring Women*, it became clear that much of what I was able to accomplish in that book owed to the challenges of those foundational teaching moments. The struggle in those classrooms was born out of the pressure between a history rooted in the archive and one applied to the present day—in other words, in the space of interdisciplinarity, with all its attendant contradictions and generative tensions.

For scholars writing the history of women in slavery, the power of the archive to erase the presence of black women demands an engagement with contemporary exclusionary structures. The historiography of gender and slavery emerges from the space of black feminism; the logic that buttresses the study of women and slavery exemplifies intersectionality in practice. Claims that histories of slavery failed to adequately consider the ways in which enslavement was a gendered practice, or that racial logic emerged from the interstices of gender as difference, owe their origin to a set of political practices aimed at dislodging the notion that one's subjugation had a single point of origin. In 1987, when Hazel Carby took John Blassingame to task over his dismissal of *Incidents in the Life of a Slave Girl* as "too melodramatic" (and thus implausible and inauthentic), she demanded that women's lives under slavery be understood as both a distinct and a core part of the fabric of enslavement.[3]

From the Combahee River Collective statement to Angela Davis's "Reflections on the Black Women's Role in the Community of Slaves," to Hortense Spillar's magisterial "Mama's Baby, Papa's Maybe: An American Grammar," black feminist theorists and activists have queried the relationship between the embodied self and the ability to address and redress archival silences. By now the claims for intersectional analysis have been well grounded—but they bear revisiting, if only to remind us of the extent to which they transformed the field of African American history and the history of slavery. There are a few different issues at play here. One is the relationship between the past and the present. Angela Davis's 1972 "Reflections" is bookended by contemporary concerns about the impact of the Moynihan report and the need for African American women to "consciously repudiate" myths about black "female castrators"—myths created in the present but fed by the past. In her response to Davis's article in the 1972 *Massachusetts Review*, Johnetta Cole wrote: "it is a well established, although seldom acknowledged fact that the questions one asks grow out of one's ideological position."[4] And yet, it is clear as she works through the piece that, for Cole, Davis's ideological position is inextricable from her embodied position: the phrase "like Black women under slavery" or "like the Black women she describes" repeat in an invocation of the link between Davis (incarcerated at the time she wrote the article) and the enslaved women whose experiences she explores.

A decade later, Deborah Gray White gestured similarly toward the silences around the history of women in slavery as produced by archival violence that "leave black women with more myths than history."[5] Indeed, after a critical overview of the scholarship on slavery (beginning with Kenneth Stampp and Stanley Elkins) and its consistent omission of women's lives, White reminds us that problems of sources for women's history are rooted in "what was and still is the black woman's condition."[6] Her identification of an endemic problem (one she does not explicitly name as racist sexism) reflected her own commitments as a politically engaged black feminist.

In addition to the connection between contemporary manifestations of intersecting oppressions and the need for restorative and revisionist historical narratives lies an issue in the critique of power: the ability to produce a set of theoretical interventions that enable us to more fully comprehend the many-headed hydra that is American race thinking. Kim Hall's *Things of Darkness* ends with an epilogue in which she locates herself as a "black feminist/renaissance scholar." She mounts a careful argument for "black feminist criticism as a methodology rather than a performance of blackness" and does so to legitimate her application of such a method to a Renaissance text as opposed to mobilizing a black feminist analysis in order to expand available black women's texts.[7] She is in conversation with the restorative work of literary critics and historians whose intent it is to expand the narrative, and thus the political, space that black women occupy—to literally place more volumes on our shelves. She is demanding, rightly, the space for black women to theorize power in many, or any, milieu; unwilling to confine her gaze to texts that are understood *a priori* as black women's texts. Her intervention is essential as it figures the study of women and slavery as one of many spaces that can be generated from a black feminist modality.

Most recently, Saidiya Hartman has launched a conversation about archives and methods, one firmly ensconced in the theoretical interventions that constitute a black feminist epistemology. In "Venus in Two Acts," Hartman finds the project of locating women in slavery as one "predicted upon impossibility ... refashioning disfigured lives ... redressing the violence that produced numbers, ciphers, and fragments of discourse, which is as close as we come to a biography of the captive and the enslaved."[8] Hartman concludes her short but generative piece with a discussion of the *failures* surrounding her effort to tell/locate the story of a girl's death on board a slave ship, which:

> Illuminate[s] the way in which our age is tethered to hers. A relation which others might describe as a kind of melancholia, but which I prefer to describe in terms of the afterlife of property, by which I mean the detritus of lives with which we have yet to attend, a past that has yet to be done, and the ongoing state of emergency in which black life remains in peril.

In this notion of the afterlife of property, Hartman gestures towards the epistemological space that I am struggling to name. It is more than simply a relationship to the archive and a presumption that to be in the archive is to inhabit a site of struggle, although it grows from that space. It is also more than the experiential dimensions of our lives in and out of the 21st-century academy, more than our individual immersion in the "ongoing state of emergency." Hartman has arrived at a place prefigured by the work of Nell Painter, who argued in "Soul Murder and Slavery" that fully assessing the impact of enslavement required grappling with its psychological toll.[9] Painter reminded us that in refusing the see the crippling impact of slavery's violence on black families, we failed to fully comprehend its costs. For those of us working now, fully unfettered by the Sambo thesis and its aftermath,[10] the willingness to grapple with the quotidian violences of enslavement feels quite normative—in our writing *and* in our classrooms. Doing so is part of our inheritance—as scholars and teachers buoyed by work initiated almost forty years ago by Angela Davis's insistence that the lives of enslaved women could tell us all something about the nature of political movements against intersecting fields of coercive power.

My work as an historian of gender and slavery has been powerfully influenced by this scholarship; but it also grows out of more prosaic struggles to incorporate the heady lessons of a black feminist positionality into the quotidian dramas of the classroom, as well as onto my bookshelves.

Notes

1. The Combahee River Collective, "The Combahee River Collective Statement," in *Home Girls: A Black Feminist Anthology*, ed. Barbara Smith (New York: Kitchen Table: Women of Color Press, 1983); *This Bridge Called My Back: Writings by Radical Women of Color* (New York: Kitchen Table: Women of Color Press, 1981); *But Some of Us are Brave: All the Women are White, All the Blacks are Men: Black Women's Studies* (New York: The Feminist Press, 1983).

2. Kimberle Crenshaw, "Mapping the Margins: Intersectionality, Identity Politics, and Violence against Women of Color," *Stanford Law Review* 43(1991).

3. Hazel Carby, *Reconstructing Womanhood: The Emergence of the Afro-American Woman Novelist* (New York: Oxford University Press, 1987), 45–46.

4. Johnetta B. Cole, "Affirmation of Resistance: A Repsonse to Angela Davis," *Massachusetts Review* 13(1972): 101.

5. Deborah Gray White, *Ar'n't I a Woman? Female Slaves in the Plantation South* (New York: W.W. Norton, 1985), 167.

6. White, *Ar'n't I a Woman?* 23.

7. Kim F. Hall, *Things of Darkness: Economies of Race and Gender in Early Modern England* (Ithaca, NY: Cornell University Press, 1995), 263.

8. Saidiya Hartman, "Venus in Two Acts," *Small Axe* 26 (2008): 3.

9. Nell Irvin Painter, "Soul Murder and Slavery," in *Southern History across the Color Line* (Chapel Hill: University of North Carolina Press, 2002).

10. Here I refer to the scholarship at pains to restore masculinity to enslaved men as the primary goal of slavery studies.

Pedagogical Crossroads: On Teaching and Conducting Research in Asian American History

Catherine Ceniza Choy

I often think of research and teaching separately. That compartmentalization is partly the result of institutional bureaucracy: my self-evaluations for promotion and merit reviews, for instance, require separate synopses of my contributions to each area. In practice, my research and teaching are deeply linked. My archival research experience influenced the use of historical documents in two undergraduate classes that I have taught regularly at the University of California (UC), Berkeley, since 2004: Introduction to the History of Asians in the United States and Filipino American History. And, in my search for teachable primary sources that depict the humanity and agency of Asian Americans, I have found materials that have shaped my current research.

After a talented undergraduate at UC Berkeley confided in me during his senior year that research seemed "mysterious," I decided that my goals as an historian-teacher would include demystifying the process. Making the decision to feature research-based learning in my Asian American history courses was easy. On a pedagogical level, having undergraduate students ill-informed about research seemed just plain wrong. On a personal and professional level, exposure to the research process during my college years enriched my life and livelihood. As an undergraduate at Pomona College, the research interests of history faculty specializing in African, Asian, Mexican American, and women's history sparked my curiosity about the history of Filipinos in the United States. Their encouragement led to my acceptance to UCLA's Minority Summer Research Program, a curriculum for underrepresented students that required participants to conduct original research. This experience laid the groundwork for my senior thesis in history, and culminated in my admission to UCLA's history doctoral program.

Having reaped the benefits of faculty links between research and teaching inspired me to forge the same links in my own career. I was able to teach upper-division students about the research process in senior seminars as well as sponsor students through various undergraduate research programs. But these programs targeted relatively few students.

In my Filipino American History course, I developed research-based learning activities and assignments that require students to locate, access, and critically analyze historical documents. An upper-division course capped at 30 students enables me to divide the students into two groups for an orientation at the Bancroft Library, where Theresa Salazar—curator of its Western Americana collection—facilitates a hands-on introduction to some of the library's special collections. One of the gems of the UC Berkeley campus, the Bancroft Library houses primary source materials on the histories of US colonization of the Philippines, holdings that are a result of university faculty's early 20th-century involvement in US colonial education in the Philippines. The library visit enables students to see the handwritten autobiography of pioneering UC Berkeley faculty member and US Philippine Commission member Bernard Moses, and the memoirs and photograph collection of David Prescott Barrows, who served as superintendent of schools in Manila, chief of the Bureau of Non-Christian Tribes of the Philippine Islands, and general superintendent of education for the islands in the early 1900s before becoming a faculty member, dean, and then president of the University of California in 1919. For my Filipino American History students, the Bancroft Library visit is a highpoint of the course.

Integrating research-based learning in my large, lower-division history course was no small feat, and involved challenges of classroom size and student preparation. The Introduction to the History of Asians in the United States course enrolls approximately 150 students. Although the Bancroft Library is also well known for its collections on the histories of the Chinese in California and Japanese American internment, I could not feasibly bring the students into the library in so many small groups over the course of the semester. Furthermore, most of the students were first-years and undeclared majors with limited research experience.

Basic exposure to historical documents was not difficult. I required students to read the book *Major Problems in Asian American History: Documents and Essays*, edited by Lon Kurashige and Alice Yang Murray, precisely to showcase the links and differences between primary and secondary sources and to emphasize the multiplicity of narratives about the past as told by various historical actors.[1] Yet the more complex question remained: How can one develop a critical engagement and appreciation of Asian American historical documents for beginning students in a large lecture course?

The Significance of Structural Teaching Support

Implementing an effective research-based pedagogy cannot succeed on passion alone; it requires institutional support. In spring 2006, I was accepted to the 2006–07 Mellon Library/Faculty Fellowship for Undergraduate Research program, an on-campus fellowship that provided the structural support enabling me to focus on this teaching objective.[2] The fellowship encouraged UC Berkeley faculty to explore creative ways to engage students by integrating research skills into the classroom. The redesign of large-enrollment undergraduate courses was the program's priority. Faculty fellows from diverse disciplinary backgrounds participated in a two-week summer institute during which we were exposed to various research-based learning assignments.

Fellows received a $2,000 stipend and individualized consultative support with experts in areas related to course implementation such as information literacy, pedagogy, library resources, educational technology, writing, course evaluation, assessment of student learning, and collaboration with graduate student instructors. My Mellon implementation team included e-learning librarian Karen Munro, humanities librarian Sarah McDaniel, Education Technology Services specialist Robert Schlick, and Student Learning Center assistant director Alex DeGuia.

I applied to the fellowship program while in the midst of teaching the Introduction to the History of Asians in the United States for the first time on campus. Past syllabi revealed that the research component of the course often involved students conducting oral interviews. I had utilized oral interview research myself in other courses, and in my first book on the history of Filipino nurse migration to the United States.[3] But in this course I wanted to focus on the critical analysis of historical documents in order to complement the research-based learning experiences in other Asian American Studies courses. This emphasis also supported my specific course goal of creating assignments that would expose students to materials related to Asian American history in the extraordinary collections of UC Berkeley's libraries, thereby contributing to their appreciation of being at a research university.

By focusing on the analysis of Asian American historical documents, my aim was not solely to have students learn about historians' foundational methodology, but perhaps even more to highlight the tremendous progress made in the previous two to three decades regarding the collection of materials documenting Asian American history *and* making those materials accessible to a broader audience. In the late 1960s, the histories and social concerns of Asians in the United States were not well known to the general public. This ignorance can be attributed in part to the erasure of a longer Asian American historical presence in the United States, a product of the mob violence that destroyed Chinese American temples, villages, and ethnic enclaves through looting and fire, and expelled Chinese Americans from the Pacific Northwest and Rocky Mountain region in the second half of the 19th century and the early 20th century. Displacement and expulsion through repatriation campaigns, alien land laws, racial segregation in housing, education, and employment, as well as outright internment and violence would also obscure the historical presence of Japanese, Filipino, Korean, and Asian Indian American experiences in the first half of the 20th century.

Widespread American ignorance about Asian American history was also an outcome of historiography, of the racist attitudes and benign neglect shared by a majority of American academics until the growth of ethnic studies programs and the emergence of the field of Asian American history in the late 20th century. Some of the Asian American history-related special collections at UC Berkeley were material manifestations of the curricular gains of student-led protests beginning in the late 1960s at San Francisco State University and UC Berkeley. Students advocated for the creation of a racially and ethnically diverse curriculum in part through the collection and preservation of multicultural histories.

The Asian American History Archival Project

The most significant new element of the course was an assignment entitled the Asian American History Archival Project. The assignment presented students with this prompt: If you could choose one document to include in the book, *Major Problems in Asian American History: Documents and Essays*, which document would you choose and why? Students were required to select one to three pages (or approximately 250–750 words) of one historical document from a course web-collection and make the case for its inclusion in one of the book's thematic chapters. The primary goal of this assignment was to give students the opportunity to shape historical knowledge by proposing and justifying a change in a college-level history text.

Since the students came from a variety of disciplinary interests, I decided in consultation with my Mellon implementation team to create what we called a "virtual stocked pond" of historical documents. Guest lectures by librarians introduced students to finding primary sources through the UC libraries' databases and the websites Calisphere (the University of California's free public gateway to more than 200,000 digitized items about California history and culture), and the Online Archive of California (or OAC, which provides free public access to descriptions of primary source collections maintained by more than 200 contributing institutions, including many digitized items). Although some students would revel in finding their own document, I imagined that many beginners would find mining through such an awesome amount of materials excessively daunting. The virtual stocked pond of historical documents leveled the playing field among students because it provided an extensive but not exhaustive list of primary sources from which to choose. I stocked the pond with source materials that directly spoke to a wide range of the themes, events, historical actors, and time periods represented in the *Major Problems* book; there was no bad choice for students to make.

Creating the virtual stocked pond was the most labor-intensive aspect of the assignment. The chronological scope of the *Major Problems* book was broad, from an early chapter on colonization, Pacific markets, and Asian labor migration before the Civil War, to a concluding chapter featuring documents and essays about Asian Americans in the 21st century. The book's contents included the experiences of many different Asian American ethnic groups, a diversity I tried to emulate in the creation of the virtual stocked pond. I also mined digitized historical documents for legibility and historical content.

The virtual stocked pond included a total of 27 online sources (22 documents and 5 sound recordings) from eight collections: the Chinese in California collection housed in the Asian American Studies section of UC Berkeley's Ethnic Studies Library; the Agricultural History Santa Cruz County series of the UC Santa Cruz's Regional History Project in UCSC's McHenry Library; the Japanese American Evacuation and Resettlement Records, 1930–1974, and the Yoshiko Uchida Papers, both housed at UC Berkeley's Bancroft Library; the K.W. (Kyung Won) Lee papers, 1972–88, held in the Special Collections of UC Davis's General Library; the Virtual Vietnam Archive of Texas Tech University's Vietnam Project; the Virtual Oral/Aural History Archive (VOAHA) of California State University, Long Beach; and the Asian/Pacific Islander Tobacco Education Network (APITEN) Records, 1990–2000, housed at the UC San Francisco's Library, Archives, and Special Collections.

While I included historical documents authored by a range of Americans in the virtual stocked pond, I made a conscious effort to include primary source materials created by Asian Americans. In the process of searching out these resources, I was struck by the paucity of digitized historical documents authored by Southeast Asian Americans and Filipino Americans. Thus, while I had not intended to use sound recordings, I chose selections from the "Cambodian Life Histories" series and the "Hmong" series of the Southeast Asian Communities collection from the Virtual Oral/Aural History Archive to include in the virtual stocked pond.

As a specialist in Filipino American history, I was not surprised that so few digitized documents featured the voices of Filipino Americans. The reason why oral interview methodology figured prominently in my first book was precisely because of the absence and the inaccessibility of a critical mass of archival material related to Filipino nurses, despite the Philippines being the world's leading sending-country of nurses and the United States the largest recipient. Furthermore, while no shortage of archival material exists relating to US colonization of the Philippines from 1898 to 1946, most materials echo the narratives of American colonial rulers, portraying Filipinos in the Philippines and in the United States in a simplistic dichotomy: as hordes of savages in need of US tutelage on the one hand, or as faceless victims of US imperialism and racism on the other. In the 21st century, significant progress has been made in Filipino American historical scholarship, but the challenge of finding accessible primary source materials that depict the humanity of the Filipino experience in the United States remains.

The most personally rewarding discovery in my search for digitized documents were two transcriptions of oral interviews—one, the life history of Filipino labor contractor Frank Barba; the other, a life history of Filipina businesswoman Apolonia Dangzalan—from the Agricultural History Santa Cruz County series of UC Santa Cruz's Regional History Project. Because young Filipino men comprised the vast majority of Filipino migrants to Hawaii and the US mainland in the early 20th century, primary source materials featuring the voices of early 20th-century Filipino women migrants are rare. Noteworthy details about Dangzalan's life abounded in the oral history transcript. She immigrated from Ilocos Sur, northwest of Manila, to Hawaii, in 1924 with her husband. Dangzalan began a long entrepreneurial career in Hawaii that continued after her migration to the US mainland. Dissatisfied with her marriage, Dangzalan divorced her husband in 1926 and proceeded to buy and manage a pool hall and restaurant in Marysville, California. She engaged in occupations that few women entered, such as labor contracting. At the time of the oral interview in 1977, Dangzalan was 81 years old and continued to work in a grocery and liquor store. She died in 1992 at the age of 96.

One of the most fascinating details about this interview, which was conducted by Meri Knaster in 1977, is the fact that it remained inaccessible to the public for almost three decades. As librarian and interview editor Irene Reti explained in the introduction to the oral history transcript: "Due to funding and staffing limitations, Apolonia Dangzalan's oral history was tucked away for 27 years in a safe at the Regional History Project."[4] Dangzalan's oral history was not published until 2004. Today, copies of the manuscript are housed in UC Berkeley's Bancroft Library, and in UC Santa Cruz's Special Collections at McHenry Library. A PDF file of the complete text and an audio clip are available online through UC Santa Cruz University Library's website.

Students Respond

After completing the Asian American History Archival Project, 109 students participated in a questionnaire about the assignment that included this request: "Can you give an example of how the research assignment has enhanced your understanding of the course material?" In response, most students pointed to an increase in their breadth of knowledge enabled by applying themes and concepts from class lectures to the analysis of historical documents: "Learned to apply concepts and ideas to analyze a primary document critically and in depth," and, "I can relate broad concepts to specific examples." They also referred to the growth of their depth of knowledge regarding specific historical topics: "In the case of Japanese internment, which my project was on, I expanded my knowledge," and, "It made me delve deeper into understanding how viewpoints differed about US Manifest Destiny." Related to these developments was a greater appreciation of historical documents: "Enabled me to think in depth about a specific topic and how different documents have different points of view on similar topics," and, "Looking up the historical context and figuring out the author and the intended audience of documents has forced me to open my mind when analyzing documents."

Implementing a research-based pedagogy transformed my own research as well. Prior to the Mellon Library Faculty Fellowship and the creation of this assignment, I had not heard of Apolonia Dangzalan and knew nothing about the existence of her oral history. Today, she is one of seven

Filipino American women I am writing about in a collection of biographical essays tentatively entitled, "In No Man's Shadow: The Filipino Woman in America." Thus, I wholeheartedly related to this student's response about the Asian American History Archival Project: "It opened new areas of Asian American history that I had yet to see."

Notes

1. Lon Kurashige and Alice Yang Murray, eds., *Major Problems in Asian American History: Documents and Essays* (Boston: Houghton Mifflin, 2003).

2. "Mellon Library/Faculty Fellowship for Undergraduate Research," http://www.lib.berkeley.edu/mellon/index.html.

3. Catherine Ceniza Choy, *Empire of Care: Nursing and Migration in Filipino American History* (Durham, NC: Duke University Press, 2003).

4. Irene Reti, "Introduction," 6 in "Apolonia Dangzalan, Filipina Businesswoman, Watsonville, California,1927–1977," interviewed by Meri Knaster and edited by Irene Reti, http://library.ucsc.edu/reg-hist/dangzalan.

The African Diaspora and the Political Imagination

Lisa A. Lindsay

For an Africanist historian working at a public university in the United States, the links between research and teaching are not always obvious. I teach classes and conduct research mostly on different continents and during different times of year. And yet the connections are significant and important, most obviously in my choice of topics, but also in my approach to those topics and the themes I emphasize in the classroom. My current research—a biography set in the 19th-century Atlantic world—has inspired my recent emphasis on personal narratives as a vehicle for historical insight and the meaning of freedom as a key question for historical understanding.

Shortly after being hired by the University of North Carolina, Chapel Hill, I was asked to teach a course on the trans-Atlantic slave trade left behind by a departing faculty member. I was at that point revising my dissertation for publication, and it had nothing to do with the slave trade. Immersed in my study of wage labor and gender relationships in colonial Nigeria, I was happy teaching modern African history and the history of women in Africa. What I knew about the Atlantic slave trade could have been covered the first day of class. Still, a junior faculty member grateful for her job does not exactly refuse a teaching suggestion from her chair, does she? In the 10 years since then, my course on the slave trade has grown from 30 to 200 students, inspired me to publish a textbook on the topic, and shaped my current research.

I am now writing a contextualized biography of an African American named James Churchwill Vaughan, whose life story forms one thread in a larger fabric of interconnections during a transformative period in Atlantic history, when slavery was abolished in the United States and colonialism began in West Africa, and when people in both places struggled over slavery, freedom, and citizenship. On the eve of the American Civil War, this freedman set out to fulfill his enslaved father's dying wish: that he should leave South Carolina for his ancestral African homeland. After moving first to Liberia, Vaughan continued further east to "Yoruba country," now southwestern Nigeria. There, he survived slave raids and political upheaval, saw the imposition of British colonialism, built a business, and founded a family. In the 1880s, Vaughan and several others led a revolt against white missionaries and formed the first independent Christian church in West Africa. Before his 1893 death in Lagos, Nigeria, he sent gold coins to a niece in South Carolina whose business had been torched by the Ku Klux Klan; his daughter and subsequent descendants maintained contact with their American relatives, to the present. Many of these Nigerian and American Vaughans have been activists, including a noted advocate for Nigerian women's education and political rights, the founder of one of Nigeria's earliest anticolonial political parties, and high-ranking US government officials. (In fact, the connection to the Nigerian women's rights activist was the bridge between my earlier work on gender and this project—I discovered her grandfather the African American in the pages of her biography.)

For the past several years, I have conducted archival and oral history research in the United States and Nigeria on Vaughan, his parents and descendants on two continents, and the contexts in which they lived. Although most of this work happens between the spaces of teaching terms and tasks, its themes and methodology have reverberated into my teaching, in the course on the slave trade and also in a new course entitled The United States and Africa.

For one thing, writing a biography has focused my attention on the ways individual life stories can bring history to life for students. For the study of the Atlantic slave trade, this approach offers a contrast to the more quantitative orientation that often dominates the field. In 1997 a team of researchers led by Prof. David Eltis of Emory University published *The Atlantic Slave Trade: A Database on CD-ROM*, a searchable compendium of data on over 27,000 slaving voyages. A second, expanded version of the database was released online in 2008 and now includes information on more than 35,000 slaving voyages. A surge of new published studies have come from this data, which offer more comprehensive information on the size, scope, and nature of the slave trade than has ever been available before. My students and I draw heavily on this material; yet, largely influenced by my own biographical research, I also aim in my classes to populate the Atlantic world with real individuals and narratives about their lives.

Part of the power of biography as a pedagogical strategy is the capacity to move students' emotions by prompting them to imagine being someone else. Focusing on individuals—and trying to trace them through the historical record wherever they might lead us—has a tendency to disrupt broad generalizations and grand preconceptions, reminding us that even seemingly vast processes, like those encapsulated in the slave trade database, were *experienced*. For example, my students read Venture Smith, author of the first North American slave narrative, describing his capture when an enemy army overran his homeland in the 1730s. After killing his father, raiders forcibly herded Smith, his mother, and other members of his community 400 miles toward the coast. "All the march I had very hard tasks imposed on me," he later recounted, "which I must perform on pain of punishment. I was obliged to carry on my head a large flat stone used for grinding our corn, weighing, as I should suppose, as much as twenty-five pounds; besides victuals, mat and cooking utensils. Though I was pretty large and stout of my age, yet these burdens were very grievous to me, being only six years and a half old."

Such personal stories can animate large-scale historical developments, making what might seem like abstract phenomena more intelligible and memorable by linking them to individuals and their experiences. It is one thing to tell students, for instance, that Africans themselves led movements against the slave trade, or that Christianity has been mixing with African religions for centuries. It is more meaningful, however, to share with them the story of Dona Beatriz Kimpa Vita. As John Thornton recounts in his book, *The Congolese Saint Anthony*, Dona Beatriz was an early 18th-century Congolese noblewoman who declared herself possessed by the spirit of Saint Anthony, gathered thousands of followers, and challenged political authorities to end the wars that fed the slave trade, before being burned at the stake for heresy and treason. Similarly, borrowing from Robert Harms' book *The Diligent*, I introduce students to Bulfinch Lambe, an Englishman taken captive in the 1720s and held as a slave in the kingdom of Dahomey. Lambe's account describes the militarization and centralization of the Dahomey state through its export of human captives, and also complains bitterly about the loss of his personal freedom—ironically, since Lambe had gone to Dahomey as an agent of the British Royal Africa Company, a major slave trading enterprise. Bulfinch Lambe's story, then, offers not only a first-hand view of a major African slave trading state, but also the lesson that there is no necessary historical connection between race and slavery.

Although the genre of biography always risks methodological individualism, tracing individuals across time and space not only joins human experience to broad historical trends, but also reveals unexpected comparisons and connections. My research on James Vaughan's story, for instance, yields two sets of revelations often missed by specialists who focus exclusively on one place. First, it reminds us that American slavery was part of a connected Atlantic world of bonded labor, one where slavery and freedom were not stark opposites but rather framed a continuum of dependency relations. Second, it illuminates the relationship between diasporic Africans and the politics of African colonialism. Both of these are themes that have come to permeate my teaching on the slave trade and relationships between the United States and Africa.

James Vaughan's emigration to Africa exemplifies a long-standing yearning for African connections to counter the genealogical alienation wrought by American slavery. But his odyssey also illuminates a wider perspective, reminding us that slavery in the United States was not as anomalous as is frequently thought. The often blurry distinctions between slavery and freedom that both predated and lasted beyond Emancipation were not aberrations in an otherwise free society; rather, they were shared features of an Atlantic world connected at least in part by a history of slavery and white supremacy. With every move, Vaughan left one slave society only to arrive in another. And in each place, his own freedom had to be carefully guarded: in South Carolina, where free African Americans like himself could be sentenced to slavery or simply spirited away, and where they could hardly own land or pursue a decent living; in Liberia, where settlers were themselves vulnerable to slavers, even as they deprived indigenous people of their own liberty; and certainly in Yorubaland, where political wars and kidnapping raids generated thousands of slaves destined for Brazil, Cuba, or servitude within Africa. Moreover, political power, social status, and the mobilization of labor depended on a range of hierarchical, extractive relations, including slavery. The British takeover of Lagos in 1861 was justified as an anti-slavery intervention. But even a generation later, most residents of Vaughan's adopted home remained slave-owners, slaves, or something resembling slaves. And as the rest of Yorubaland fell under British colonial control—a process begun and largely completed during Vaughan's four decades there—even people nominally "free" were increasingly unable to claim political citizenship.

What, then, is the meaning of *freedom*? Historians such as Rebecca Scott, Thomas Holt, and Frederick Cooper have asked this question in a variety of contexts, and it animates my study of James Vaughan. The question has also become central to my teaching on slavery and the slave trade. By looking at different features of slavery in different contexts, my students and I note its similarities and variations over time and place. We compare slavery to other forms of labor organization such as indentured servitude, pawnship, or sharecropping. Which forms became targets for reform in certain times and places, and which were considered perfectly legitimate? Moreover, even when slavery was abolished, what freedom would actually entail was very much an open question. Did freedom mean political citizenship, physical safety, and access to land, as many freedpeople hoped, or did it provide a new context for disfranchisement and subservience? What, in people's hopes and imaginations, did free societies look like?

If my research preoccupation with the meanings of freedom has come to inform my teaching on slavery and the slave trade, so has the insight, key to my own scholarship, that the African diaspora did not move solely from Africa to the Americas, and that the circulation of people of African descent had important effects in Africa itself. Southwestern Nigeria became home in the 19th century not only to its indigenous population, but also to "repatriates" from Sierra Leone, Brazil, and Cuba, where they or their parents had been slaves. Liberia attracted thousands of African American settlers; some, like James Vaughan, struck out for other parts of Africa. How did these transnational migrants—the "reverse" African diaspora—affect Africa? During a period in which slavery persisted, white supremacy flourished, and colonial rule intensified, diaspora Africans were notably successful in gaining, and also challenging, political authority. Black Atlantic migrants could draw on their own initiative, experiences from multiple contexts, and dispersed connections in their struggles for dignity and security.

Prompted by this insight, I devote a section of my course on The United States and Africa to back-to-Africa movements by African Americans. These included not only 19th century settlers in Liberia, but also African Americans looking for a homeland outside the influence of the American Colonization Society, as well as later, sometimes temporary, migrants such as W.E.B. DuBois and Maya Angelou. By examining the journeys and outlooks of such diasporic travelers (memorably recounted in James Campbell's book *Middle Passages*), my students consider their visions of freedom, how their American and African experiences related to those visions, and what impact they had in Africa. Informed by my own research on a back-to-Africa migrant, I see this "reverse diaspora" as part of a larger migratory pattern in African American history as well as important for understanding some African developments. Moreover, when we study people who crossed boundaries like the Atlantic Ocean, we see that African peoples over time have traveled and worked both within and outside of national frameworks, prompting our observation that the best way to understand historical developments, and people's historical experiences, is not always through the lens of the nation-state.

As an Africanist historian, my basic goals in the classroom and in my scholarship are three-fold: to familiarize Americans with Africa (and thus to de-exoticize the "dark continent"); to illuminate connections in the past and present between Africa and other parts of the world; and to provoke comparisons that suggest the range of possibilities open to people as they build and shape their societies. How have people defined *freedom* and worked to make it real? On what basis have people identified with one another and worked to build communities; or, under what circumstances have they failed to find common ground? Ultimately, these are questions about the political imagination: can other people's stories allow us to envision not only their world, but the ways their preoccupations might cast light on ours? In my research and my teaching, I suggest that the answer is yes.

Bringing Communication Back In: Rethinking the Teaching-Research-Service Distinction

Jeffrey Wasserstrom

When writing up annual reports on what we've done in the past year, as well as preparing materials for tenure and promotion files, academics are routinely asked to divvy up the things we do into three differently marked boxes. We are expected to draw a clean line between activities that relate to "teaching" and those that relate to "research," while hiving off from both the activities that qualify as "service." Accomplishments of each variety matter, though we all know that not all are created equal. At research universities of the kind in which I've spent my career, the word "teaching" comes first (the phrasing is "teaching, research, and service"), but we are socialized quickly to think of the middle pursuit as the one that really counts. Applicants can easily get tenure with good teaching and excellent research; they will have a harder or even impossible time doing so with stellar teaching and research that is merely good. The traditional phrasing of the triumvirate applies best to "service," as we receive cues that it matters least. What kinds of cues? Well, with teaching and even more so with research, there is an effort to assess quality (prestige of publication venues, numerical scores on student evaluations), while with service the focus tends to be on the *amount of time* spent serving on this or that committee.

Early in my career, I didn't think much about the divvying up process, as I found it relatively easy to place many of my activities into the three boxes. So long as I didn't probe the issue, it seemed natural to see a basic distinction between what I did in the classroom, what I published, and my committee work. Occasionally, I was confused even then.

In the early 1990s, I was encouraged to apply for grants to bolster my "research" portfolio. To secure such grants, I wrote out plans of activity that felt a lot like committee reports (an obvious form of "service"). This was especially true with the most prestigious of my grants, since I worked closely with the associate director of a center in preparing the application (which felt akin to being part of a great small committee). Moreover, though securing the grant was deemed a "research" accomplishment (and got me released from teaching for a semester in order to do some reading and writing, hence helping me to show more indications of scholarly productivity), it also funded a workshop (service? research?), which I co-directed with the center's associate director, someone with whom I also edited a working paper series (service? research?). One could say that grants even of this sort fit neatly into the research pile, since they are awarded in part as acknowledgment of stature, which reflects *past* publications. But probed too closely, this argument does not quite wash, as the same track record can elicit invitations to speak at a public library (which would count as "service"). Over time, the number of instances in which I was doing something that seemed to belong in more than one category or at the border between them multiplied.

This was partly due to the fact that my activities were unusual (at least for a historian of my generation)—from writing for magazines to helping curate an exhibition of political posters—and partly due to shifts in the academic and publishing worlds (new media ventures sometimes problematize old categories of assessment). But it was also due to my thinking harder about some things that I had not really thought about before. Take a lecture at a public library or for a Rotary Club or a group of high school teachers in an outreach event: all are quintessential "service" activities, but I also see each as a form of "teaching." Preparing for them draws on lectures given in college classrooms as well as "research" conducted to add a special dimension to the specific presentation. The questions I get from the audiences at these events—like the questions I get from students—can then lead me to explore new angles in my research. And so on.

Turning from the questions I am asked to those I ask myself, here are some related to the teaching, research, and service trio that I began to ponder. Where should I put a workshop that had sessions open to the public (service); involved graduate students I mentored (teaching); and led to a scholarly volume (research)? How should I categorize a think piece that was largely about recently published monographs, but was neither a straightforward book review (of the sort I'd been told should go in the service category) nor a highly specialized research article (no question where those go), but in which I had included material from archival digging of my own to expand on my commentary on works by others? And what about consulting for a documentary film? There, my expertise was sought because of my research, but the product was to be of general interest, hence working on it seemed a form of service. What the filmmakers wanted most, it turned out, were suggestions for how to convey ideas about complex aspects of history that would remain true to the archives but could be communicated in an easily digestible manner for those without specialist knowledge. That felt a lot like prepping for class, or "teaching."

I now find the divvying up process utterly maddening, fundamentally out of step with what I think of as the arc of my intellectual and professional life. It is true that my career has been idiosyncratic, and novel forms of new media keep making their mark on the landscape, but I can't help wondering if these specific factors have simply brought some always-latent confusion to the surface. I am baffled in any case to even begin to categorize my work with *China Beat*, the group blog that a few of us launched at the University of California, Irvine, which ran from early 2008 until mid-2012. It would seem a classic "service" enterprise—designed as it was to share ideas with a general audience—but the brainstorming sessions linked to it made up part of the training that Ken Pomeranz and I provided our students (which felt like "teaching"), and it served as a venue for trying out ideas that were just beginning to percolate into research projects. (Ken and I, and no doubt others, saw blog posts pave the way for and spur work on scholarly articles.)

If the three categories that once seemed watertight have turned out to be very porous, with what might we consider replacing them? I don't know precisely how to make assessment exercises any easier for others, but here are some ways that I've begun to differentiate things for myself. Some of my activities that benefit each of the three realms can be described as "hunting and gathering" (e.g., the search for an evocative quotation or image, whether used to back up a point in a scholarly article, to read or show in class, or to integrate into a talk for a community group). Another set involves "figuring out what the audience knows" (so as to ensure that I make the most of the time I have with the people with whom I am trying to communicate—on the page or in person, in a classroom, a museum, or during a committee conference call—to tell them something they will find new and interesting). Then there is "polishing the prose"—my strategies for conveying ideas and information most effectively (whether coming up with a hook for the opening of an opinion piece, deciding on the mix of references to work by others and quotations from original sources in a scholarly article, or a joke to tell at the start of a public presentation or survey class lecture). Often, rather than think about "teaching," "research," and "service," I now find it more useful to break up my activities into "discovering," "preparing" and "communicating," dividing my time between digging for information, texts, and images, trying to make sense of what I have found, and figuring out how to express what I think I know.

Re-reading this essay, I'm left wondering about things that get left out of the picture when intellectual life is seen as a set of purposive activities in which the interaction between a scholar and an audience is presented running in just one direction. What's missing? The fact that teachers can learn as much from their students as their students learn from them (while we "mentored" the students who contributed to China Beat, the two graduate students editing it basically taught us how to blog); the randomness of some intellectual breakthroughs (some of my recent scholarly writing has seen me grappling with *1984* and *Brave New World* as lenses through which to view China—an idea that came to me while preparing for an invited lecture at a college that happened to have assigned the latter book to all incoming freshmen); and the spill-over effect that experiments in one area can bring to another (my teaching and research experience made me a better consultant to those filmmakers, but working with them changed the way I teach and left me with new questions to ask of sources in my research). Another way to put this is that while it is all well and good to say that one loves to teach (or dig into archives, or write, and so on), what makes the difference in having a satisfying life in my profession really comes down to keeping the love of learning (and, yes, I have even learned things from committee work).

What would an annual report look like if we were asked to focus not on what we had published in journals, taught in the classroom, or done in committee sessions, but on what we had learned over the course of a year? And not just learned—a final thought that falls squarely into the Feedback Loop—but also then figured out how to communicate.

About the Authors

Antoinette M. Burton is a professor of history Bastian Professor of Global and Transnational Studies at the University of Illinois, Urbana-Champaign. She is the author of *A Primer for Teaching World History: Ten Design Principles* (Duke, 2012) and the editor of *The First Anglo-Afghan Wars, 1839–1919: A Reader* (forthcoming, Duke University Press).

Teofilo F. Ruiz is a professor of history at the University of California, Los Angeles; his publications include *From Heaven to Earth: The Reordering of Castilian Society, 1150–1350* (Princeton University Press, 2004), *Spanish Society, 1400–1600* (Longman, 2001), *Crisis and Continuity: Land and Town in Late Medieval Castile* (University of Pennsylvania Press: Philadelphia, 1994), and *The City and the Realm: Burgos and Castile in the Late Middle Ages* (London: Variorum Reprints, 1992).

Steve Johnstone is a professor of history at the University of Arizona, and is the author of *A History of Trust in Ancient Greece* (University of Chicago Press, 2011), and *Disputes and Democracy: The Consequences of Litigation in Ancient Athens* (1999).

Carol Symes is an assoicate professor of history at the University of Illinois at Urbana-Champaign, and author of *A Common Stage: Theater and Public Life in Medieval Arras* (Cornell University Press, 2007), which received the Herbert Baxter Adams Prize from the American Historical Association.

Shefali Chandra is assistant professor of history, international studies, and women, gender, and sexuality at Washington University in St. Louis, and author of *The Sexual Life of English: Languages of Caste and Desire in Colonial India* (Durham: Duke University Press, 2012).

Laura E. Nym Mayhall is associate professor at The Catholic University of America, and author of *The Militant Suffrage Movement: Citizenship and Resistance in Britain, 1860–1930* (Oxford University Press, 2003) and co-editor, with Ian Christopher Fletcher and Philippa Levine, of *Women's Suffrage in the British Empire: Citizenship, Nation and Race* (Routledge, 2000).

Mary Jo Maynes is a professor of history at University of Minnesota, and the co-author, with Ann Waltner, of *The Family: A World History* (Oxford University Press, 2012), and, with Jennifer L. Pierce and Barbara Laslett, *Telling Stories: The Use of Personal Narratives in the Social Sciences and History* (Cornell University Press, 2008).

Ann Waltner is a professor of history and the director of the Institute for Advanced Study at the University of Minnesota; she is also the author of *The Family: A World History*, with Mary Jo Maynes, (Oxford University Press, 2012).

Bianca Premo is an associate professor of history at Florida International University, and the author of *Children of the Father King: Youth, Authority, and Legal Minority in Colonial Lima* (University of North Carolina Press, 2009), and co editor, with Ondina E. González, of *Raising an Empire: Children in Early Modern Iberia and Colonial Latin America* (University of New Mexico Press, 2007).

Kathi Kern is a professor of history at the University of Kentucky, and the author of *Mrs. Stanton's Bible* (Cornell University Press, 2001).

John Ramsbottom is a professor of global and historical studies at Butler University.

Jennifer L. Morgan is professor of history and of social and cultural analysis at New York University, and author of *Laboring Women: Gender and Reproduction in the Making of New World Slavery* (University of Pennsylvania Press, 2004).

Catherine Ceniza Choy is a professor of ethnic studies at the University of California, Berkeley, and author of *Empire of Care: Nursing and Migration in Filipino American History* (Duke University Press, 2003), and *Global Families: A History of Asian International Adoption in America* (NYU Press, 2013).

Lisa A. Lindsay is an associate professor of history at the University of North Carolina at Chapel Hill and the author of *Captives as Commodities: The Transatlantic Slave Trade* (Pearson, 2007) and *Working with Gender: Wage Labor and Social Change in Southwestern Nigeria* (Heinemann, 2003). She is also co-editor, with Stephan F. Miescher, of *Men and Masculinities in Modern Africa* (Heinemann, 2003).

Jeffrey Wasserstrom is a professor of history at the University of California at Irvine, and the author of *China in the 21st Century: What Everyone Needs to Know* (Oxford University Press, 2010 and 2013 editions), *Global Shanghai, 1850–2010* (Routledge, 2009), and *China's Brave New World: And Other Tales for Global Times* (Indiana University Press, 2007).